MENTORING
ADULT
LEARNERS

A Guide for Educators and Trainers

The Professional Practices in Adult Education and Human Resource Development Series explores issues and concerns of practitioners who work in the broad range of settings in adult and continuing education and human resource development.

The books are intended to provide information and strategies on how to make practice more effective for professionals and those they serve. They are written from a practical viewpoint and provide a forum for instructors, administrators, policy makers, counselors, trainers, managers, program and organizational developers, instructional designers, and other related professionals.

Editorial correspondence should be sent to the Editor-in-Chief:

Michael W. Galbraith
Florida Atlantic University
Department of Educational Leadership
College of Education
Boca Raton, FL 33431

MENTORING ADULT LEARNERS

A Guide for Educators and Trainers

By
Norman H. Cohen

KRIEGER PUBLISHING COMPANY
MALABAR, FLORIDA

Original Edition 1995

Printed and Published by
KRIEGER PUBLISHING COMPANY
KRIEGER DRIVE
MALABAR, FLORIDA 32950

FROM A DECLARATION OF PRINCIPLES JOINTLY ADOPTED BY A COM-
MITTEE OF THE AMERICAN BAR ASSOCIATION AND COMMITTEE OF
PUBLISHERS:

This Publication is designed to provide accurate and authoritative information in regard to the subject matter covered. It is sold with the understanding that the publisher
is not engaged in rendering legal, accounting, or other professional service. If legal advice or other expert assistance is required, the services of a competent professional person should be sought.

Library of Congress Cataloging-In-Publication Data

Cohen, Norman H. (Norman Harris), 1941–
    Mentoring adult learners : a guide for educators and trainers / by
Norman H. Cohen.
        p.   cm. — (The professional practices in adult education and
human resource development series)
    Includes bibliographical references (p.   ) and index.
    ISBN 0-89464-850-0 (alk. paper)
    1. Mentors in education.   2. Adult education.   3. Continuing
education.   I. Title.   II. Series.
LC5225.M45C64   1995
374—dc20   94-36430
                                                           CIP

10 9 8 7 6 5 4

CONTENTS

PREFACE

Mentoring programs are viewed as an increasingly important source of learning for adults whose personal, educational, and career development can benefit from meaningful relationships with experienced professionals. However, experts who study the mentoring of adults as a *learning experience* generally agree that the professional staff who serve as mentors often have inadequate conceptual and empirical preparation for the realities of the mentoring relationship, whether in higher and adult postsecondary education, counseling, human resource development, government, or business.

The overall purpose of *Mentoring Adult Learners: A Guide for Educators and Trainers* is to provide pragmatic guidance to those who assume responsibility for the mentor role so that they can function as more *significant influences* in their mentoring relationships with adult learners (as students or employees). The book includes two versions of the Principles of Adult Mentoring Scale—one for postsecondary education (PSE) and one for business and government (B&G)—which offer professionals a self-assessment instrument that can reveal their behavioral competencies in the mentor role.

Institutions can plan and operate mentoring programs which create interpersonal conditions that actively encourage the development of significant adult mentoring relationships (which would have never "naturally" occurred). Organizations investing in such sponsored mentoring programs can therefore increase the probability of contributing to the nurturing of mentor-mentee relationships that produce positive rather than marginal or even negative results. Properly understood and conducted, the mentoring program can then realize its potential to offer a powerful learning experience for adults.

In viewing mentoring as a process of learning, this work attempts to accomplish four main objectives:

1. To directly connect the relevant research base of adult mentoring theory and practice to the actual world of evolving mentoring interaction by stressing real life application

2. To link essential knowledge from the fields of adult psychology and applied interpersonal communication skills to the behavioral challenges of mentor-practitioners faced with establishing and maintaining mentoring relationships

3. To provide a self-assessment instrument, for use by professionals who have assumed the responsibility of mentor to adult learners, that will encourage their reflection about mentoring relationships and enhance their comprehension of and proficiency in the role of mentor

4. To offer specific guidance on the planning and operating of the sponsored/organized mentoring program

The intended audiences for this book include two-and four-year college faculty, counselors, administrators, staff at postsecondary educational institutions, professionals who manage a variety of intern training programs, and human resource development specialists in business and government. The book is also aimed at social service and nonprofit sector personnel responsible for managerial and employee training and development, as well as professors and graduate students in higher and adult education who wish to conduct research in mentoring.

Mentoring Adult Learners: A Guide for Educators and Trainers has nine chapters. The introductory chapter clarifies the value of mentoring relationships in adult development. Next, it introduces the transactional (collaborative) process of learning and connects the important issue of risk to the mentoring of adults in education, business, and government, and reviews other critical mentor concerns such as trust, timing of comments, and confrontive interaction. Finally, the chapter introduces the six interpersonal functions of the mentor role, and then places them in the context of the developmental phases of a mentoring relationship.

Chapter 2 invites the reader to take a version of the Principles of the Adult Mentoring Scale. It raises the issue of mentor-mentee compatibility with respect to factors such as mentor authority, gender, ethnicity, and age, and encourages a sensitivity to differences which could influence the outcome of mentoring relationships. The chapter also examines in more detail the interpersonal application of the six core mentor behavioral functions, provides facts about scale development, and explains how to interpret scale scores. (Significant issues relevant to mentor-mentee differences are expanded as topics in Chapter 9).

In Chapter 3, the *relationship emphasis* behaviors of the mentor role are explained as essential in establishing the foundation upon which a significant mentoring relationship will be constructed. This function is viewed as a focus on the mentor's skill in conveying, through active, empathetic listening, a genuine understanding and acceptance of the ideas and emotions expressed by the adult learner. The purpose of the relationship emphasis function is defined as that of creating a psychological climate of trust which allows adults to honestly share and reflect upon their personal experiences as learners.

The *information emphasis* behaviors of the mentor role are examined in Chapter 4. This particular function is presented as that of directly requesting detailed information from and offering specific suggestions to adult learners about their current plans and progress in achieving personal, educational, training, and career goals. The major point of this chapter is to highlight the importance for the mentor of offering advice which is based on accurate and sufficient knowledge of each unique adult learner.

In Chapter 5, the *facilitative focus* behaviors of the mentor role are described as guiding adult learners through a reasonably in-depth review and exploration of their interests, abilities, ideas, and beliefs relevant to education, career, and current work situation. The objective of the facilitative focus function is explained as that of assisting adult learners to consider alternative views and options while reaching their own decisions about attainable goals.

The *confrontive focus* behaviors of the mentor role are presented in Chapter 6 as behavioral skills required to carefully challenge adult learners' explanations for or avoidance of decisions and actions important to their educational and career development. The confrontive focus function is explained as a strategy designed to help adults attain insight into unproductive strategies and behaviors, and to evaluate their need and capacity to change. The risks to the relationship created by confrontation as a deliberate intervention are also reviewed, since its constructive use by the mentor is assumed to require considerable proficiency.

Chapter 7 provides an explanation of the *mentor model* function as that of self-disclosing appropriate life-experiences as a participant role model in order to personalize and enrich the relationship. The primary objective of the sharing dimension of mentor model behaviors is presented as that of motivating adult learners to take reasonable risks and to continue overcoming difficulties in their own journey toward educational and career-related goals. An important distinction is also made between the mentor's and the mentee's personal style of confronting and resolving problems.

In Chapter 8, the *mentee vision* function of the mentor role is described as stimulating mentees' critical thinking with regard to envisioning their own educational and career future, and to actively continuing their personal and professional development. Mentee attitudes about their own personal possibilities in education, business, and government are reviewed, especially with regard to the apparent impact of such self-perceptions on their vision as adult learners. The mentee vision function is presented as helping adult learners more independently take initiatives as they manage personal changes and transitions, and negotiate through educational, workplace, and life events.

Finally, Chapter 9 concludes by providing a proactive model for planning and operating the sponsored mentoring program, with a primary focus on the importance of carefully recruiting and orienting mentors and mentees, as well as on the value of conducting ongoing training seminars. In addition, other major points are covered which could influence the quality of the evolving mentoring relationship, such as mentor authority over the mentee, gender, ethnicity, age, and the impact of length and frequency of sessions. Also, the significance of the mentoring "context" is reviewed as a factor in mentor-mentee interaction.

Mentoring is portrayed as a dynamic interaction which requires mutual commitment to truly evolve into a satisfying and meaningful learning experience. If properly approached, the mentor and the mentee should each take pleasure in the enriching interpersonal exchange of *offering and receiving* which is the essence of the adult mentoring relationship.

ACKNOWLEDGMENTS

I am a very fortunate member of the "sandwich" generation.

I have parents, David and Mollie, and children, Jonathan and Jill, from whom I receive sound advice. My wife, Sheila, also offers patient and astute suggestions. They have all been invaluable resources on whom I could depend as well for emotional support.

This book reflects all of their voices, not just my own.

My mentor and now friend, Michael Galbraith, has been a source of inspiration and knowledge. His voice is also very much a part of this work.

Mary Roberts, senior editor at Krieger Publishing Company, provided astute guidance that contributed to the clarity of the book.

My other companions, Jasmine, our gentle Labrador, and Carmel, our wise calico cat, who enriched our family before she recently succumbed to diabetes after a valiant fight, mentored our entire family. I am sure their voices are in this book.

And to all of my students who constructively influenced me as I tried to positively influence them, thank you for allowing me the opportunity to make a difference. Your voices are on every page.

THE AUTHOR

Norman H. Cohen is an associate professor of English at the Community College of Philadelphia. He received his B.A. (1964) in English from Washington College, his M.A. in English (1968) from Temple University, and his Ed.D. in adult education (1993) from Temple University.

Dr. Cohen's primary interests have centered on the use of adult psychology to promote adult learning in a variety of educational, business, government, and social organizations. His current research pursuits involve the development of one-to-one mentoring models of learning as well as the application of the mentoring approach to small group and classroom interaction. Cohen's work, which has mainly focused on the adult learner (18 to 55+), is also now being extended to the below-18-year-old population.

As an active lifelong learner, Cohen has presented his ideas for consideration at various seminars and conferences. The Principles of Adult Mentoring Scale is now being used by many institutions as part of their efforts to provide continuing education for mentors.

With Dr. Michael Galbraith, Dr. Cohen is coeditor of *Mentoring: New Challenges and Visions* (1995).

Dr. Cohen consults with a wide range of academic, business, health care, and government organizations to establish and maintain proactive mentoring programs.

CHAPTER 1

Mentoring Adults

The importance of mentoring relationships in adult development has been documented for centuries. The actual word *mentor* can be traced to the *Odyssey* and derives from Odysseus' implicit trust in Mentor, to whom he delegated complete responsibility for raising his son Telemachus. This ancient story portrays the essence of the classic mentoring relationship as the power of an older, wiser, experienced person to dramatically influence a younger protégé's intellectual and emotional growth during the important transition into adulthood. Mentor entered our contemporary language as a description of a nonparental, competent, and trustworthy figure who consciously accepts personal responsibility for the significant developmental growth of another individual.

As we approach the year 2000, the theory and practice of mentoring, when understood as a highly significant and productive interpersonal process of learning, can offer much to professionals who are committed to assisting adults in their pursuit of educational, training, and career goals. As an orientation to the mentor role, this chapter will first provide an overview by answering a fundamental question: What is mentoring? Then, seven specific aspects of mentoring will be examined:

1. The differences between mentors and other helping professionals

2. The mentor as a partner on the mentee's journey

3. The mentor's influence on learning

4. The mentor's timing of feedback, especially confrontive

5. The mentor's attention to the issue of trust with respect to a mentee's readiness for confrontation

6. The concept of mentoring as a transactional process of learning

7. The phases of the mentoring relationship

WHAT IS MENTORING?

Mentoring as a behavioral activity refers to the one-to-one relationship that evolves through reasonably distinct phases between the mentor and the adult learner (student or employee). As used in this book, an adult learner refers to any person 18 years of age and above who enters into a mentoring relationship to develop, separately or in combination, his or her personal, educational, or career potential. Of course, mentoring can and does occur with persons younger than eighteen, as can be observed in the important relationships formed between socially conscious citizens and disadvantaged youth. And while much of the information in this text can be adapted to the below-18-year-old population, the primary focus has been on those adult learners already functioning in a postsecondary education or employment-related environment.

A metaphor proposed by Daloz (1986) of the mentee as an adult learner who has consciously undertaken a developmental *journey* helps to clarify three key functions provided by the mentor: support, challenge, and vision. Daloz refers to the experience of learning enacted within the mentoring relationship as a complex and evolving process of interpersonal interactions, and he describes mentors in education as committed to "promoting such generic abilities as critical thinking, the capacity for empathy, the power to take diverse perspectives, and the will to take positive actions in a tentative world" (p. 206). Daloz views mentors as assuming a role which allows them to *"align themselves in relation to their students . . .* Mentors are, thus, *interpreters of the environment"* (pp. 206–207). He concludes by focusing on the relational process of learning: "For more than any other factor, it is the partnership of teacher and student that finally determines the value of an education. In the nurture of that partnership lies the mentor's art" (p. 244).

THE MENTORING ROLE

An increasing body of literature relevant to mentoring now clearly supports the view of the mentor role as comprised of a number of interrelated behavioral functions that are combined in the mentoring relationship to assist each adult learner. The role of the mentor advocated in this book as most appropriate for and effective with adults is defined as that of the professional-as-mentor who demonstrates observable interpersonal communication skills in six behavioral functions.

Each of these particular functions will be explained in Chapter 2, but a brief description regarding their significance should clarify the essential purpose:

1. Relationship Emphasis, to establish *trust*

2. Information Emphasis, to offer tailored *advice*

3. Facilitative Focus, to introduce *alternatives*

4. Confrontive Focus, to *challenge*

5. Mentor Model, to *motivate*

6. Mentee Vision, to encourage *initiative* (Cohen, 1993)

In addition to a focus on specific mentor behaviors, the value of modern mentors should also be understood in reference to the wide sociocultural context in which they might exert a positive influence.

As concerned professionals, mentors can actively help other adults to develop their own unique personal, educational, and career potential across the social landscape of academic, government, and business environments. Mentors make a difference primarily because their competent mentoring behaviors enable them to transmit the essential quality of *trust*. This quality is a characteristic of adult educators who are perceived as truly committed to the development of adult learners, regardless of their gender, age, or ethnicity, or whether the mentors and mentees are officially labeled as instructors and students or managers and employees. Mentors who are viewed as creditable persons can thus more effectively interact with adult learners for the purpose of enhancing their intellectual and affective (emotional) development.

According to the recent literature of education, business, and government, the mentoring phenomenon has achieved a significant status. Mentoring is viewed as a powerful influence in promoting "retention and enrichment" (Jacobi, 1991, p. 505) in postsecondary educational settings (Daloz, 1986; Galbraith, 1990, 1991a; 1991b; Schlossberg, Lynch, & Chickering, 1989). The importance of mentoring relationships as a factor in personal maturation and successful adult adjustment to numerous life roles is as well a general theme of the adult development and counseling literature (Brookfield, 1986; Gilligan, 1982; Levinson, Darrow, Kline, Levinson & McKee, 1978; Merriam, 1984; Sheehy, 1981).

In the context of business and industry, many expert observers believe that while management practices are often out of touch with our contemporary workplace and marketplace, studies of planned mentoring programs in business continue to reveal their positive contribution to career enhancement as demonstrated by personal adjustment, satisfaction, and professional achievement (Bova, 1987; Kram, 1985; Marsick, 1987; Zey, 1984). Also, the success of mentoring programs designed to promote career development and to groom managers for senior positions in government has been well documented (Murray, 1991).

Differences between Mentors, Academic Advisors, Personnel Specialists, and Counselors

Some general descriptions are now offered to distinguish mentoring from other person-to-person helping functions, such as the academic advisor, counselor, and personnel specialist, since persons new to mentoring may have already been influenced by these other "roles." To be effective in the behavioral role of mentor, whether in postsecondary education, business or government, professionals will need to have clear perceptions about themselves as *providers of assistance*, just as mentees will need to have clear expectations about themselves as *receivers of assistance*.

The *complete mentor role* has been defined as containing six core functions: Relationship Emphasis, Information Emphasis, Facilitative Focus, Confrontive Focus, Mentor Model, and Mentee Vision. In addition, the mentor's commitment to assist in the developmental growth of another person is described as requiring a reasonably substantial personal investment over an *extended time frame*, even if the mentee is referred at different points for supplemental help to others, such as counselors, faculty, administrators, or managers. By fulfilling the responsibilities of each behavioral function, the mentor in postsecondary education, business, and government attempts to create a synergistic effect which allows the evolving mentoring relationship to become "larger" than the six separate mentor components. It is this combination or blend which ultimately creates a meaningful mentoring experience for the mentee.

By contrast, the typical academic advisor in postsecondary education is generally not expected to engage in frequent or lengthy meetings, and often limits the topics of discussion to academic content-focused concerns, such as progress toward the degree, requirements, grades, the selection of courses, and sometimes actual scheduling. Moreover, the academic tasks associated with advising relationships are often considered to be short-term and definite rather than evolving and developmental, and students in postsecondary education are not assumed to require frequent or recurring meetings with their advisors, especially if they have already decided on courses and curricula.

If students have problems which impact on their academic performance, the academic advisor usually refers them to another staff member or department, such as counseling, tutoring services, or financial aid. Often, in these case the students are not expected to return for another appointment, or if they do, they concentrate on resolving problems relevant to immediate academic topics of concern. The objective of a genuine *developmental* relationship occurring as a result of the interaction between the academic advisor and the student is not presupposed because their contact is recognized as minimal. The establishment of an ongoing relationship comparable to the complexity of mentor and mentee interpersonal interaction is therefore not usually viewed as a stated purpose of the typical academic advising program in postsecondary education.

Using the six mentor functions as a guideline, the academic advisor's primary interest would normally be located within the information component, with facilitation and mentee vision as a possibly included but more touched on aspect of the interaction. Also, the confrontive approach could be involved but limited, for example, to clear-cut situations, such as students who insisted on registering for courses without having the proper prerequisites or who requested course loads or selections which were clearly not sensible based on their prior records.

In business and government, the advisor role would normally be fulfilled by someone from the personnel or human relations area, although union representatives, including those in postsecondary education, could also serve as mentors. The topics covered could vary from employee requests for information about opportunities for training and career advancement, to dealing with perceived personality conflicts between co-workers, to investigating allegations of unfairness which are causing nonmanager-manager conflicts.

Such designated personnel can certainly be assumed to have a good faith interest in offering legitimate assistance to all of the participants, but they would probably need to reference policy and procedure as an integral aspect of resolving issues of significance. Also, they would often be required to refer employees to other staff within the hierarchy when possible disciplinary actions were involved, or to outside mental health professionals for help with concerns such as as alcohol or substance abuse, or other emotional and psychological problems seriously impacting on work performance.

In general, the personnel advisor role in the business and government context would focus on the information emphasis component, with some facilitative and even (careful) confrontive elements included if employee interest or behavior so indicated. Staff representing personnel or human relations departments would also be much more cautious about offering employees *direct* suggestions with regard to decisions, and often even indicate that they were only explaining or stating the available official positions or options. In the case of a pending adverse action, they might offer comments specially phrased to emphasize the following point: "I'm not here to *tell* you what to do," or "You'll really have to make your *own* decisions." Though a personnel specialist may in fact be of significant assistance to an employee, the short duration of their interaction should also be viewed as pragmatically precluding the development of a substantive personal relationship.

An important distinction relevant to counselors in postsecondary education, or personnel specialists in business and government with counseling credentials and responsibilities, would be their formal preparation as *trained* helping professionals. Assuming the usual education and experience, counselors would have been exposed to a background that encompassed most of the behavioral skills and many of the goals described in the six mentor functions. Although there are clearly different schools of thought about counseling interventions, in general, as members of a counseling or personnel department, counselors would usually need to be prudent about explicitly venturing into the mentor model dimension, as well as careful about being too confrontive with students or employees.

The counseling or personnel specialist helping approach described here is usually based on the premise that the staff members will not function as continuing participant role models, though there are instances when counselors will engage in relatively long-term relationships with students. Counselors or staff from personnel therefore generally enter into their interactions from the perspective of limiting comments about their significant personal experiences. Such an approach appears sensible, since the motivational value of their selective self-disclosure would be very difficult to gauge if based only on minimal mutual contact. Of course, if the organization which the counselor or specialist represents had objectives consistent with the goals of the true mentoring program, then certainly the mentor model function could be appropriately included in these interpersonal interactions.

There is another factor to consider. The recipients of such

information could be very inexperienced, and a serious but unanticipated problem could occur as a result of this directly shared self-disclosure. Students or employees could easily misinterpret the message, and then be unintentionally misled because they literally infer that specific *solutions* to their own problems were being directly advocated by means of these illustrative stories. In the absence of specific information about a student or employee, a counselor would risk offering generic explanations that might or might not apply, and thus be viewed as reducing individual needs and problems to relevant, but essentially procedural, details.

To be described as engaged in mentoring, the counselor or personnel specialist would need to consciously attempt to integrate the specific mentor model function, as well as to be concerned about a number of other factors, including the frequency, length, and depth of issues covered in meetings. The evolution of person-to-person interaction into an ongoing relationship comparable to the mentoring model would thus involve serious attention to fulfilling the selective but meaningful sharing of experience component that is built into the mentor role.

Although most trained counselors could skillfully include the mentor model function, they would first need to believe that this sharing/modeling dimension was consistent with their own role. Generally, of course, more probability exists in postsecondary counseling of establishing a schedule of recurring and longer term meetings than in business or government, and the mentor model function could become part of the generic counseling department approach if there were consensus by the professional staff.

With respect to *productive* confrontation, a major concern should always be the potential for negative reactions created by the limited contact between counselors and students or personnel specialists and employees. Certainly, counselors or personnel staff could, and might need to, engage in directly confrontive behaviors with students or employees. And if, as in some counseling department models, the contacts were initially established as more long-term interactions, then the confrontive facet could also be a proper intervention. But unless the resources of the organization are devoted to such realistic concerns as allowing for sufficient time and frequency of meetings, then the construction of the basic *foundation* of trust, information, and facilitation would be most unlikely between the participants—and confrontation more likely a strategy that creates more problems than it solves.

Without a reasonably solid interpersonal base, counselors and specialists need to place clear limits on their initiatives in pointing out serious discrepancies or inconsistencies. Well-intentioned motives could still result in a marginal or even terminated helping relationship because of the (often understandable) inability of the student or employee to handle and benefit from immediate and directly confrontive behavior.

Confrontation is difficult enough to transform into positive assistance in a properly supportive climate between individuals who have some established relationship, so the implications of confrontive behaviors between persons who are essentially strangers must always be carefully weighed.

In postsecondary education, business, and government, *mentor* attempts to influence mentees within the directive dimension of the total mentoring experience are assumed to be appropriate and positive. However, students or employees who are not in mentoring relationships may view themselves as in very different life and work situations than those who have chosen to become mentees. Mentor initiatives which are proper within mentor-mentee interaction could thus be viewed by such individuals as too aggressive or even manipulative when they occur outside the boundaries of mentoring, as in the usual academic advising setting or in the type of counseling generally practiced in education or in business and government.

The legitimate differences between the mentor and those in the other helping functions—whether academic advisor in postsecondary education, personnel specialist in business and government, or counselor—should be openly discussed so that the important behavioral distinctions, content-appropriate issues, and goals relevant to all of the participants in the *mentoring relationship* are clarified. Such understanding will promote the realistic interaction that is essential if those who offer assistance, and those

who benefit from it—the mentor and the mentee—are to successfully recognize and deal with the constraints, and to meaningfully
explore the possibilities, of their social environment.

MENTORING AS A PARTNERSHIP

The partnership approach to mentoring should be understood
as an expansion rather than a contraction of a major principle of
adult education: the belief that student-centered teaching is at the
center of truly significant adult learning. The legitimate recognition that students should be actively involved as both planners and
participants in their own learning continues to have a deservedly
important impact on the theory and practice of adult education
and, by extension, of adult mentoring.

However, the behavioral influence of practitioners directly
involved with adult learners on a frequent basis must certainly be
viewed as a significant developmental force on the learning which
occurs for the mentee. And the professional in the mentor role
should rightfully attempt to maximize this potential for positive
influence within the defined boundaries of the mentoring relationship, and to fulfill as many of the mentoring functions as are required to assist the progress of adult learners. A mentor, though,
cannot simplistically and automatically equate the *fact* of mentoring
sessions with important learning occurring for a mentee; to do so
could minimize the fundamental difference between significant
and insignificant mentor influence on a mentee within the mentoring relationship.

Moreover, expecting the mentee to become magically enfran-
chised to independently proceed simply because a topic or goal has
been discussed is comparable to the view of proficiency as a bestowed competency rather than a process of learned behavior. This
problem is sometimes overlooked in our 1990's "age of empower-
ment," with its often rapid shift or delegation of decision-making
responsibility—without adequate attention to *learning*—to those
traditionally in the employee and even student role.

The art of mentoring, of course, requires maintaining a reflective balance so that appropriate mentor influence does not tip over into either inappropriate mentor "control" or unrealistic "hands off" mentee expectations. The mentor's proper intent to empower the mentee must be tempered with an awareness of the mentee's *own* balance as an adult learner engaged in the trial-and-error activities, reflection, and self-correction normally characteristic of the learning process itself. A respect for and understanding of a unique mentee's learning curve is essential if the mentee is to develop as a confident adult learner.

MENTOR INFLUENCE

The power of both teacher and manager-centered learning to reinforce the situational dependency of adult learners needs to be counterbalanced by a proactive effort to establish an adult-centered (student or employee) environment. This appropriate attempt to create a more balanced relationship should not unrealistically shift attention from either the obvious or subtle responsibility of the mentor, as a rational, empathetic, and experienced partner to positively influence the direction and quality of learning for the mentee. As noted by Baskett, Marsick, and Cervero, (1992), professionals generally need help to "understand the processes by which they use practical knowledge in their practice contexts. This calls for a departure from the prevailing assumptions imbedded in CPE (continuing professional education) practice, that is, what the learner does is more important than what the instructor does" (p. 114).

In fact, with regard to the reality of mentoring as a learning experience, the central issue is not *will* the mentee be influenced, but *how?* Even Rogers's (1961) formulation of client-centered therapy, a philosophy and methodology of practice that attempted to free an overly controlled patient from the hands of the therapist-healer as "expert," never suggested the inappropriate perception of the therapist as exerting little or no behavioral influence on the outcome of the therapy, or how could one justify any therapeutic intervention at all? As Dewey (1938) also wisely noted with respect to the influence of the teacher on the learner:

The belief that all genuine education comes about through experience does not mean that all experiences are genuinely or equally educative. Experience and education cannot be directly equated to each other. For some experiences are mis-educative. Any experience is mis-educative that has the effect of arresting or distorting the growth of further experience. (p. 13)

MENTOR TIMING

The mentor's comments will not be made in a relational vacuum, and a significant aspect of mentor influence will depend on timing. As an integral part of attaining proficiency in the six behavioral functions of the complete mentor role, a very real concern for the mentor must be the timing of comments offered to the mentee, especially those focused on confrontive issues. The general framework proposed for the mentoring relationship stresses the importance of establishing an *early* psychological/emotional baseline foundation of trust with the adult learner as a prerequisite to promoting meaningful personal reflection and appropriate self-disclosure in later interaction. Those relationship and information mentor behaviors relevant to developing the trust between the mentor and mentee necessary to sustain the probable confrontive interaction in the mentoring relationship therefore assume vital importance.

TRUST AND CONFRONTATION

A mentor will be faced with a decision created by another concern related to timing—the "readiness" of the mentee to benefit from the challenge of a constructive critique at a particular phase of the relationship. Confrontive interaction, though sometimes a necessary mentor behavioral function, is usually associated with risk to the foundation of the mentoring relationship, and therefore should be considered as an intervention that requires astute mentor awareness and skill during all phases of the evolving interpersonal relationship. In the initial phases, before some meaningful trust has developed between the adult learner and the mentor, con-

frontation should be viewed as an especially high-risk mentor behavior, to be employed when mentee decision-making time is limited and consequences to the mentee are serious.

READINESS OF THE MENTEE

The complexity of mentor and adult learner interaction pre-
cludes a simplistic checklist approach of "what to say when" statements, but the mentor must be aware of the extent to which the
mentee is *receptive to and able to benefit* from legitimate challenges
at any point in the relationship. A mentor should pay primary attention, however, to enhancing the process of relational and informational development with the mentee before directly challenging
any adult learner's ideas, beliefs, or facts; this awareness of timing
and trust as related factors will often prove to be a critical component in establishing and maintaining a successful mentoring relationship.

Mentor verbal comments in general are therefore likely to
exert an effective or ineffective influence on the mentee based on
three interrelated factors: (1) the combination of perceptual and
factual *accuracy* of insights offered, (2) the prior foundation of
developed *trust*, and (3) the careful *timing* of the relevant confrontive remarks. Well-intentioned constructive feedback will be most
practically beneficial if the mentee is reasonably ready to consider
and work on applying the insight and information offered by the
mentor.

There are also differences in the probable impact on the mentee with regard to the specific type of comments offered. For example, suggestions for improving behavior (such as poor listening
or excessive arguing) are likely to be interpreted as more personally threatening than comments about insufficient knowledge, and
thus could contribute more often to pronounced defensive responses.
The mentor's skill at defusing the overreactions of a mentee will
prove to be a valuable component at such moments in the mutual
information exchange. Since the mentee determines to what extent any critique provided by the mentor is accepted and constructively utilized, the more rational the mentee's reactions, the higher

the probability that the mentor's intention to offer positive assistance which makes a difference will be realized.

MENTORING AS A TRANSACTION

The mentoring relationship has been defined as a "transactional process" and a "tool to enhance learning (that) can be found in a variety of settings" (Galbraith & Zelenak, 1991, p. 126). The core of mentoring, when viewed as a transactional process of learning, is the focus on collaborative participation and mutual critical thinking and reflection about the process, value, and results of jointly derived learning goals established for the mentee. An important component of mentoring also stressed by Galbraith (1991b) is that of *risk taking*, which he views as an integral part of the transactional process. He elaborates on the relevance of risk in promoting meaningful learning:

> A true learning transactional process engenders three types of risk taking: the risk of commitment, the risk of confrontation, and the risk of independence. A commitment to the ideals and actions of a transactional process is a risk. To submit to the transactional process suggests that facilitators and learners run the risk of self-confrontation and change. It involves the extension of oneself into new dimensions and territories of involvement and action. (p. 5)

With regard to the power of the instructional role in either academia or business, Knowles (1970) stressed over twenty years ago that the "behavior of the teacher probably influences the character of the learning climate more than any other single factor" (p. 41). The mentor's *direct and indirect* impact on the conditions of the mentoring environment, and thus on the opportunities for mentee learning, must be recognized as a key component of the developing experience. The mentor-mentee relationship, whether it occurs in education, business, or government is a learning activity essentially created for the benefit of the mentee, with the mentor functioning as a guiding but not controlling influence on the mentee's choices and goals. The mentor therefore assumes responsibility for promoting a transactional process of learning, which

involves active involvement with a mentee as a collaborative partner in learning.

PHASES OF MENTORING

Mentoring should be understood as a dynamic and interactive process that occurs within phases of an evolving experience
for the mentee and the mentor. Scholars and practitioners have
consistently emphasized the importance of comprehending the developmental nature of mentoring relationships whose aim is personal, educational, and career growth. The concept of *developmental phases*—early, middle, later, and last—in the mentoring
model, however, should be primarily used to identify the basic issues and objectives of each phase and to suggest the type of mentor behaviors usually most appropriate for each stage of the relationship.

Of course, there may well be legitimate opportunities for the
mentor to incorporate some of the factual content from one phase
into another. In fact, the astute mentor should approach the evolving mentoring relationship as a developmental sequence which requires a keen awareness of the *pace* of the mentee's progress as an
integral factor in learning. In considering each mentee as a unique
adult learner, the mentor must be alert and flexible, as well as prepared to make adjustments for differences in individual maturity
and learning style, which, for instance, certainly could account
for one mentee progressing reasonably quickly, and another rather
slowly, through an anticipated sequence of competency development. Learning should not be viewed as an inflexible path of development that all mentees will travel at the same cognitive or affective speed or move though with the same tangible results.

The six essential behavioral functions of the mentoring role
as they occur within the four major phases of a mentoring relationship can be interpreted as a general blueprint of an evolving
interpersonal relationship, which will include mentor and mentee
adaptation and modification. The framework of mentor functions
viewed within distinct phases is thus proposed to explain the general developmental process of mentor-mentee interaction, rather

than as a rigid sequence of necessarily step-by step progression. A mentor must be especially aware, however, of counterproductive initiatives. For example, although a mentor may properly rely on and reference the accumulated information and experience regarding a specific mentee in the later phases of their relationship, mentor behaviors (such as confrontive) introduced too early into the mentoring sessions, when support might be the primary need of a mentee, could clearly be an unproductive mentor action.

In essence, mentor-mentee interpersonal development can be described as containing an *early phase*, in which the mentor emphasizes *relationship* behaviors with the mentee to establish the foundation of trust required for personal understanding, nonjudgmental acceptance, meaningful dialogue, and relevant self-disclosure. During the *middle phase*, the mentor emphasizes (as a positive and reasonably safe psychological climate is created) the information accumulation and exchange component to ensure factual understanding of each unique mentee's concerns and goals.

The mentor, in the *later phase*, explores (after the critical relational and informational dialogue conditions are created) the mentee's interests, beliefs, and reasons for decisions through *facilitative* interaction, and also very carefully and selectively engages (as necessary) in the *confrontive* dimension to elicit an appraisal by mentees of their own self-limiting strategies and behaviors. Finally, in the *last phase*, the mentor actively functions as a *mentor model* who directly motivates mentees to critically reflect on their goals, to pursue challenges, and to be faithful to their own *mentee vision* of chosen personal, educational, and career paths.

Mentoring viewed as a transactional process of learning thus highlights the interpersonal interaction between a mentor and an adult learner as characterized by collaborative participation in the educational experience and mutual reflection about the process and results of learning. Moreover, the blend of specific mentor behavioral competencies considered essential for the nurturing of a mentoring relationship is understood as occurring within a reasonably distinct, though certainly not walled off, framework of phases.

In this method of learning, mentee assumptions are examined, relevant changes and attainable goals are identified, and appropriate actions are encouraged to promote individual growth. Although this approach to mentoring is grounded in an educational model, the concept of face-to-face interaction between professional staff and adult learners as an evolving process also has an established history in adult counseling models (Hammond, Hepworth, & Smith, 1977; Miller & Musgrove, 1986; Rogers, 1961; Schlossberg, Lynch, & Chickering, 1989; Thurston & Robbins, 1983).

SUMMARY

This chapter has reviewed the purpose of mentoring, the significance of the mentor role, the important distinctions between mentor interaction and other types of helping interventions, the collaborative nature of the mentoring relationship, the relevance of trust and timing, especially when confrontive positions are involved, the view of mentoring as a transactional process of learning, and the various phases of the mentoring relationship.

Chapter 2 introduces the Principles of Adult Mentoring Scale (PAMS) which was developed as a self-assessment instrument for use by educators and managers who have consciously assumed the responsibility for developing mentoring relationships with adult learners. It has two versions—PSE for postsecondary education and B&G for business and government. The instrument provides specific information mentors can use to evaluate their behavioral competencies in the role of mentor, and it can assist professionals to become active and vital participants in the mentoring experience.

CHAPTER 2

Assessing Your Mentoring Effectiveness

You are invited to complete the postsecondary education (PSE) version of the Principles of Adult Mentoring Scale (see Appendix A) or the business and government (B&G) version (see Appendix B) before you continue reading the chapter.

Scale scores should assist you in establishing a reference point from which to view your individual proficiency in the complete mentor role, whether as educator or manager. Your own mentor profile can be interpreted as a reasonably accurate reflection of your *actual* (based on prior experience) or *probable* (based on little or no experience) mentoring style with adult learners. This information will also enable you to identify more personally with the six mentor functions that will be examined in this chapter.

It is important to note that for the participants—mentor and mentee—the value of the mentoring relationship may be interpreted as a legitimately different experience, and thus contain separate personal meaning, in Erikson's well-known observation, for each as a "universe of one." As a mentor, self-knowledge relevant to your own influence on mentee development is obviously very important, since an implication of the scale is that mentor competency scores indicate both *negative* as well as *positive* impact on a mentee as a result of experiencing a mentoring relationship. And the assumption, of course, is that enhanced mentor self-awareness and skill can release the creative energies which will allow more of a "universe of two" to occur, and thereby increase the interpersonal potential within the mentoring relationship.

Although the scale was primarily created to offer individual mentors a mirror in which they might privately view their public role as mentors of adult learners, it (and the related explanatory material) can also be used by both the researcher and the mentor-practitioner to analyze, understand, and improve general professional mentoring practice in education, business, and government (Cohen, 1993).

PRINCIPLES OF ADULT MENTORING SCALE

Personal assessment and self-directed learning are critical to the continuing professional education of lifelong learners, especially in our rapidly changing culture (Beder, 1989; Brookfield, 1986). But professionals currently have limited opportunities for assessing their probable or actual competency as mentors of adult learners (students or employees) of any age, although a few commercial instruments are available (Alleman, 1982; Gray, 1991) which measure facets of the mentoring relationship. In fact, after a comprehensive review of the adult mentoring literature, Jacobi (1991) referred to the "continued lack of clarity about the antecedents, outcomes, characteristics, and mediators of mentoring relationships despite a growing body of empirical research" (p. 505). She concluded that "Mentoring research also needs valid and reliable instruments" (p. 512).

As conscientious practitioners reflecting on their own developing competencies (Schon, 1987), mentors would certainly need to be cautious about solely relying on unchallenged individual experience as a reliable and valuable teacher, because it lacks the reality check dimension offered by other relevant feedback. One important purpose of the scale, therefore, is to provide mentors with a means of assessing their interpersonal behavioral skills, especially those competencies that appear essential for mature and productive interaction across a wide spectrum of people labeled as mentees.

Although the Principles of Adult Mentoring Scale clearly proposes that a core of mentor functions underlies the complete mentor role, the subtlety of mentoring interaction must not be viewed, however, as simply reduced to a "one behavior fits all" approach to assisting adult learners. Another critical factor influencing the mentor's contribution will be the ability to recognize and respond to the implications of important mentor-mentee differences, such as age, gender, ethnicity, socioeconomic background, and current life situation. Mentor competency in the behavioral functions and sensitivity to differences are therefore both viewed as necessary to the relationship. A more detailed examination of those issues which could influence the value of mentoring relationships will be provided in Chapter 9.

With respect to to the conceptual approach behind the scale, the unifying theme was succinctly captured in the book *Facilitating Adult Learning: A Transactional Process* (Galbraith, 1991 a). Galbraith and Zelenak (1991) had argued that mentoring should be included within the transactional framework of adult education because "Learners are viewed as partners in the educational encounter who assume responsibility for their own learning and behavior" (p. 17). The theory advanced in their work of the mentoring relationship as a unique partnership in learning—a *transaction* between the mentor and the adult learner—served as the theoretical foundation from which the mentor role, general behavioral functions, and specific item statements of concrete mentor-initiated actions were developed for use in mentor self-assessment.

Scoring and Interpreting the Scale

As the mentoring relationship evolves, the mentor should attempt to fulfill the responsibilities of the role by demonstrating effectiveness in all of the mentoring behavioral categories. Each of the six discrete mentor functions, which together constitute the complete mentor role, is explained below.

Relationship Emphasis

The mentor conveys through active, empathetic listening a genuine understanding and acceptance of the mentees' feelings. The purpose is to to create a psychological climate of trust which allows mentees (who perceive mentors as listening and not judging) to honestly share and reflect upon their personal experiences (positive and negative) as adult learners in education or the work-place.

Information Emphasis

The mentor directly requests detailed information from and offers specific suggestions to mentees about their current plans and progress in achieving personal, educational, and career goals. The purpose is to ensure that the advice offered is based on accurate and sufficient information of individual mentees' differences.

Facilitative Focus

The mentor guides mentees through a reasonably in-depth review and exploration of their interests, abilities, ideas, and beliefs relevant to academia or the workplace. The purpose is to assist mentees in considering alternative views and options while reaching their own decisions about attainable personal, academic, or career goals.

Confrontive Focus

The mentor respectfully challenges mentees' explanations for or avoidance of decisions and actions relevant to their development as adult learners in education or to their career development in the workplace. The purpose is to help mentees attain insight into unproductive strategies and behaviors and to evaluate their need and capacity to change.

Mentor Model

The mentor shares appropriate life experiences and feelings as a role model to mentees in order to personalize and enrich the relationship. The purpose is to motivate mentees to take necessary risks, make decisions without certainty of successful results, and continue to overcome difficulties in their own journey toward educational and career goals.

Mentee Vision

The mentor stimulates mentees' critical thinking with regard to envisioning their own future and to developing personal and professional potential. The purpose is to encourage mentees to function as independent adult learners, to take initiatives to manage change, and to negotiate constructive transitions through personal lifestyle and workplace events.

The brief descriptions offered above of the six mentor functions are expanded in Appendix C, which provides a detailed explanation of the purpose and specific behaviors of each function.

What Do the Scores Mean?

The scale primarily highlights the behavioral proficiency of the mentor as a significant influence on the mentee. Self-assessment of their own competencies, much like the value offered by a personal compass, is assumed to help mentors better locate themselves on the map of their mentoring relationships, so that they can contribute as much as possible to the meaning of the journey for the mentee.

Mentors should interpret the overall score as a general indicator of competency. In the integrated or complete role, the mentor fulfills multiple responsibilities by maintaining a relatively balanced mentoring relationship. Each of the six specific behavioral functions reveals the mentor's expertise in distinct and highly important components of the adult mentoring relationship.

Although the mentor can certainly prove to be a significant, if temporary, figure in the life of the mentee, as the approach to scoring indicates, the concept of the mentoring relationship also assumes that the scores reflect estimates of possible productive as well as unproductive mentor influence on the mentee. This does not imply that mentors can simply use the Principles of Adult Mentoring Scale to infer a direct cause-effect connection between their own behaviors and the responses of their mentees, or that mentors can or should literally control the outcomes of mentoring interaction. Rather, mentors should use the scores to become more alert to the impact of their specific behaviors on mentees.

Of course, as has been noted, the concept of the complete mentor role, which is defined as the blend of all six mentor functions, is also based on an evolving relationship of mentor-mentee interpersonal interactions which can be influenced by other issues (see Chapter 9).

In addition, both versions of the scale reflect differences in the social environment that could impact on the realistic pursuit of such mentee interests as personal, educational, training, and career development. Version PSE focuses on the concerns (and resources) expected in education, with more emphasis on personal/academic content in the educational environment, and version B&G focuses on the concerns associated with mentoring in business and government, with more emphasis on training/career content in the workplace.

In general, regardless of context, high mentor scores in confrontation which are not balanced with high scores in relationship should certainly trigger an alarm. A mentor could be very adept at and invested in a confrontive style of interaction. But this behavioral intervention, when employed in a situation in which the mentee is too vulnerable or emotionally off balance, could also become an interpersonal disaster. If critical factors such as trust and timing are ignored, the probability of doing the mentee more harm than good could be much increased.

By contrast, low scores in confrontation but high scores in relationship could indicate a relative avoidance of the need to point out discrepancies. Such an approach might suggest that the mentor is indirectly contributing to the continuance of unproductive mentee strategies and behaviors, because the unqualified positive nurturing could also be interpreted as tacit approval by the mentee if appropriate questions are not raised.

With respect to actual scoring, please note that in the "Instructions for Scoring and Interpreting" section of each scale (Appendixes A and B), the scores generated by the answers to the 55 item statements of the Principles of Adult Mentoring Scale are recorded on scoring sheets which contain the same factors and items, except that "Student Vision" is used on the scale for postsecondary education (PSE), and "Employee Vision" appears on the sheet for business and government (B&G).

Also, both scoring sheets (PSE and B&G) assign scale items to specified mentor functions, utilize a numerical point value of 1 to 5 to establish individual mentor function scores, and provide a grand total to determine the overall mentor score.

As you read Chapters 3–8, it is important to remember that each of the six mentoring functions is presented as a separate and self-contained behavioral competency, and the composite created by the blend of all six is labeled the contemporary mentor role. Although *Mentoring Adult Learners* is organized around the principle that effective mentoring should be viewed from the perspective of mentor behavioral skills, this approach is not meant to imply that being of genuine assistance to another person can be reduced to only an issue of observable behavior, any more than the opposite suggestion that having good intentions alone can be taken at face value as all that is necessary to meaningfully assist others.

A more realistic and mature understanding certainly offers compelling evidence that when interpersonal competency and sincere intentions are combined, the opportunity is clearly increased for realizing a more ideal mentoring relationship. Such a climate allows mentees to fulfill their individual potential as they explore and decide what is best for them on the paths of their own journey. An observation offered by Rogers (1961), which emphasizes the difference between imposing and assisting, helps to clarify this point:

> If I see a relationship as only an opportunity to reinforce certain types of words or opinions in the other, then I tend to confirm him as an object—a basically mechanical, manipulable object. And if I see this as his potentiality, he tends to act in ways which support this hypothesis. If, on the other hand, I see a relationship as an opportunity to "reinforce" *all* that he is, the person that he is with all his existent potentialities, then he tends to act in ways which support *this* hypothesis. I have then—to use Buber's term—confirmed him as a living person, capable of creative inner development. Personally, I prefer this second type of hypothesis. (pp. 55–56)

In terms of genuine relevance for either the new or the practicing mentor, this book assumes that the potential for continuing self-assessment, reflection, and competency development offered by the explanation of the mentor role, the descriptions of the specific behavioral functions, and the view of mentoring as an evolving and collaborative relationship will be of more significance than the reference point value of initial scores.

And certainly, in addition to the ideas suggested in this work, each of you as a mentor will rely on your own unique intelligence, creativity, and seasoned judgment to assist mentees in utilizing the mentoring experience as an important opportunity for learning during their journey as adult learners.

SUMMARY

This chapter has addressed points relevant to how the Principles of Adult Mentoring Scale (versions PSE and B&G) can be used to help a mentor, whether working in education, business, or government, to assess and improve the behavioral proficiencies required to establish and maintain a successful adult mentoring relationship. The topic areas covered also included a review of the basic mentor competencies, the six mentor functions, and the scoring and interpretation of scale scores.

Those interested in technical informationless will find it in Appendix D, which provides data regarding scale construction and statistics.

It is now time to turn to Chapter 3 and examine a central component of the mentor role—the relationship function.

CHAPTER 3

Establishing Mentoring Relationships

The effort to promote competency in specific mentor behaviors is not intended as advocacy of a professional costume of verbal and nonverbal behavior into which the mentor suits up in preparation for a mentoring session. Instead, the purpose of proposing that an individual establish and maintain proficiency in the complete mentor role is to highlight the type of *mentor behavioral profile* with the most potential for generating mentee learning; it is not to suggest a mechanical, superficial, and predetermined response. As Brookfield (1990) observed with respect to group interaction:

> One of the most damaging mistakes facilitators can make in leading discussions is to pretend to a personality they don't possess. . . . This is not to say that one should not pay attention to how one might better communicate in a discussion. One of the best teaching improvement exercises is to watch oneself leading a discussion group on video tape. The scope for improvement rapidly becomes evident. (p. 199)

The mentor role that has been identified is therefore advocated as primarily valuable because certain observable mentor behaviors clearly appear to increase the probability of establishing and maintaining a successful adult mentoring relationship.

However, this recognition of a definable role for the mentor is not intended to reduce the value of mentee-initiated learning. In fact, the mentoring experience should be viewed as a significant opportunity for the mentee to practice the adaptive behaviors required of any maturing adult who must come to terms with the personalities of other relevant adults. Although the mentor cannot be "all things to all mentees," the successful mentor will most likely be someone who performs competently in the role of mentor based on what is currently known about the positive and negative influences of particular interpersonal behaviors.

As with most relationships of significance, the nuances of the early relational connection between the participants often establishes a qualitative tone which can be of a special importance. Of course, the first encounter between the mentor and mentee can occur in a variety of ways, from an unplanned and spontaneous event (not recognized as an incipient mentoring relationship) to the planned match of an organizationally-sponsored program. While there also will be variations in the details of the beginning interaction, the initial phases of the mentoring experience involve several mentor behaviors—the relationship and information emphases—that are critical in establishing the *trust* which is essential between the mentor and mentee if the meetings are to gradually evolve into a meaningful mentoring relationship.

The interpersonal skills of the mentor are therefore of vital significance in establishing the early *relational* and *informational* foundation which constitutes the underlying framework of adult mentor-mentee interaction. The mentor can then build a substantive mentoring relationship which appropriately incorporates the *facilitative, confrontive, mentor model, and mentee vision* dimensions.

Although this aspect of interaction has important implications for sustaining a productive relationship during the entire lifespan of mentoring, in the early developmental stages the relationship emphasis should be viewed as containing long-term power for influencing the quality of the interpersonal connection for the mentee. The relationship component primarily involves the conscious attempt by the mentor to convey through *empathetic behaviors* both an understanding and an acceptance of the mentee's emotional situation, even if the mentor would differ greatly in his or her own probable reactions to similar perceptions and events. In an early psychological climate which allows the mentee to be heard without being judged, the probability that the mentee will also share relevant self-reflective introspection about personal and professional concerns with the mentor is thereby increased.

Five different mentor behaviors have been identified as contributing to an especially positive empathetic influence on the evolving relationship.

1. Practice responsive listening (verbal and nonverbal behaviors that signal sincere interest).

2. Ask open-ended questions related to expressed immediate concerns about actual situations.

3. Provide descriptive feedback based on observations rather than inferences of motives.

4. Use perception checks to ensure comprehension of feelings.

5. Offer nonjudgmental sensitive responses to assist in clarification of emotional states and reactions.

These important behavioral skills, which are often associated with the helping professional, clearly apply as well to the mentoring model of interaction. Each will be examined separately.

RESPONSIVE LISTENING

The verbal and nonverbal behaviors often labeled as "listening" are of major significance in communicating the accurate perception that the mentor is genuinely concerned about the mentee as a unique individual. The mentee will understandably respond to and rely on the observable behaviors of the mentor as the indicator of internal intentions or motives, and often will be influenced by the lightening strike of first impressions, a not always reliable but still powerful force in determining the early direction of the mentoring relationship.

If the mentor has noble intentions and objectives but an interpersonal listening style that is viewed by the mentee as distant or aloof, then the mentee may quickly withdraw into the protection of silence or limited response. While a mentor may self-correct this negative early impression, the mentee's perception of the mentor as a responsive listener will enhance the development of the important initial phases of the mentoring relationship and help to counterbalance any baggage of personal insecurities and doubts that the mentee may carry into the session. Factors not directly within the mentor's arena of prior influence would then have a higher probability of being properly addressed rather than of too easily turning into potentially overly defensive reactions which could detract from the purpose of mentoring.

This type of responsive listening will be examined as a combination of two separate but interrelated categories: nonverbal and verbal behaviors.

NONVERBAL DIMENSION OF LISTENING

The power of nonverbal behavior—eye contact, facial expression, voice tone, gesture, and posture—to positively or negatively impact on the interpersonal relationship can occur at almost any point in the evolving relationship. In the formative stages the nonverbal influence has an especially negative potential to over ride a mentee's judgment *before* a rational decision can be formulated about the probable value of the mentoring experience. This concern about mentor behavior in the early relationship emphasis phase is not intended to create an unproductive self-consciousness, but rather to point out that mentor nonverbal communication is a factual reality which cannot be underestimated. Certainly, there is a difference between attempting to project an idealized or perfectionist persona as a mentor and the attainable expectation of reasonably consistent and effective mentor nonverbal competency.

An important early goal, therefore, of the astute mentor will also be to help the mentee recognize how overly defensive mentee reactions to legitimate nonverbal feedback can interfere with and even prevent learning, especially when the context of learning requires feedback as an integral component of the learning process and interaction. If a mentor, for example, is actually in the habit of intensely listening by crossing arms and leaning backwards, away from other persons, such a combination of movements *could* suggest a negative response or attitude to some mentees. But the mentee can also be instructed in the art of more careful nonverbal reading of the mentor, and by extension, thus benefit by learning to more maturely read other people who may also be future sources of information and assistance.

Certainly, the mentor should still operate on the assumption that it is only when the mentee can accept critique-based feedback that the mentor's comments will make a difference. But the mentor should not assume that personal mentor nonverbal behavior must be so idealized that the mentee can be allowed to engage in microreactions to every movement or to make the issue of the mentor's nonverbal behavioral style the central concern, when in fact such a focus could clearly serve as a substitute for other, more important mentee problems.

Eye Contact

Eye contact has long been acknowledged as a critical fact of interpersonal communication. Substantial research (Weaver, 1993) indicates that the development of the trust dimension in human interaction is significantly influenced by unspoken interactions that are quickly interpreted as approval or disapproval messages received through the medium of eye contact. The mentor can therefore utilize a positive pattern of visual interaction to reinforce the climate of psychological support and thereby strengthen the bond of trust between them. Relatively frequent eye contact itself communicates the attitude of friendliness, at least initially, much more rapidly than even carefully chosen words.

The mentor, however, is not being asked to wear a perpetual happiness mask, nor is a generic prescription for eye contact that would cover all mentoring interactions now being proposed. Instead, the alert mentor can rely on what traditional wisdom advocates as a powerful signal—that warmth in the eyes which directly contributes to an atmosphere of acceptance and concern.

Facial Expression

The face can obviously convey a wide range of emotions (Devito, 1990; Weaver, 1993). Mentor facial expression should reinforce the psychological comfort zone of support in a mentoring relationship and encourage the mentee to feel accepted and understood.

Both friendly and serious mentor facial expressions are likely to be a natural response to the mentee's range of concerns and issues, but the underlying message consistently communicated should be that of approval of the mentee as a person even if there is disagreement regarding the mentee's decisions and actions. Without viewing the face as a medium to be employed like a facial puppet show for suggesting internal attitudes, the astute mentor should endeavor to use facial expression to mirror concern and support for the mentee as a baseline condition inherent in the mentoring relationship.

The distinction suggested by the ancient concept of distinguishing between "the sin and the sinner" is not simply an overstated semantic point. While dramatic differences in mentor-mentee problem-solving strategies may sometimes strain mentor patience and even blur the separation of the mentee as a person from the mentee as an adult learner, the mentor must still guard against the unintentional communication of nonacceptance of the mentee as a person within the mentoring relationship.

Certainly, there will be occasions when the mentor's face will appropriately reflect the intense concentration relevant to the serious topic under discussion. However, the mentor also must remember—when appropriate as well—to communicate the positive attitude associated with facial expression that is relaxed and reasonably tension-free—the almost magical quality associated with the smile of acceptance. The nonverbal power of the mentor to communicate openness must be reflected outwardly on the face and not remain latent as unrealized intention in the brain.

Voice Tone

The quality of warmth or coldness expressed by the tone of voice contributes a significant positive or negative dimension to interpersonal relationships (Devito, 1990; Weaver, 1993). Although there is clearly a continuum of voice tone that ranges from the opposites of highly friendly to highly unfriendly, the mentor should attempt to communicate a baseline tone of reasonably and clearly friendly—but not necessarily dramatic or solicitous—interest in the mentee's development.

The speed at which a nonverbal element such as perceived warmth or coldness can transform the meaning of the interaction must also be recognized, and if the legendary cold shoulder of disapproval is communicated through the mentor's voice, then the positive potential for constructive dialogue within the relationship may be seriously limited. Conversely, the accepting attitude of positive concern demonstrated by a warmer tone of voice can certainly enhance the essential trust dimension of the mentoring relationship, and thereby increase the mentee's willingness to explore difficult personal, educational, or career topics.

Gestures and Posture

The overall physical appearance of the mentor will contribute to the mentee's general impression of comfortableness as an accepted and valued person in the relationship (Devito, 1990; Weaver, 1993).

The mentee will often initially view the mentor as an authority figure (the association with past negative-to-positive experiences with authority will vary). To mitigate the possible negative perception of traditional authority figures as judges who critically (in a dogmatic or overly stern manner) evaluate the competence and performance of those persons they are judging, the mentor can attempt to utilize posture and physical gestures that convey an attitude of acceptance, especially within the behavioral function of confrontive emphasis. Certainly, the more relaxed the overall physical appearance of a mentor, the greater the probability of triggering a less tense and more rational mentee response to the issue under discussion.

Although the mentor should not unrealistically expect to eliminate the mentee's normally defensive reactions to legitimate, well-intentioned, and even skillfully communicated constructive critiques, the mentor can attempt to reduce the degree of mentee defensiveness in the situation. For example, pointing a finger at a mentee while offering a comment or raising an arm with the hand palm outward in a "be silent" gesture, could easily be interpreted as a condescending or accusatory message.

Any mentor body language, therefore, that promotes the momentum of the mentee toward constructive thinking and action and away from simply defensive responses to mentor behaviors will be an important contribution to the overall positive responsiveness of the mentee. Some examples of such attract-repel behaviors are: the openness suggested by leaning slightly forward instead of away from (distancing), open arm gestures rather than the negative impression of crossed arms (nonacceptance), or a hand under the chin while fixing the eyes directly at the mentee (as if the mentee is being judged) rather than relaxed head movements (nodding to show understanding).

To mitigate an obviously unintended impact, a mentor aware of his or her individual nonverbal traits could openly state to a mentee that certain behaviors, such as excessive or practically no gesturing, are in fact personal characteristics and then suggest to the mentee that if an apparent mixed message is being received, it is appropriate for the mentee to inquire—that the mentor will not be offended.

This type of ambiguous interpersonal message can present an opportunity for the mentor to communicate to the mentee that even concerned helpers, like mentors, still have their own legitimate personalities (even with training and credentials in behavior) and are not cardboard figures. The mentor should therefore openly indicate that as an important aspect of mature learning, mentees must also become aware of and deal with their *own* reactions to the nonverbal habits of others with whom they will frequently interact.

The value of this experience for the mentee can sometimes be less than obviously apparent at the exact moment of verbal and nonverbal interpersonal contact. Although a mentee may very much benefit from this aspect of mentoring, evidence of the attainment of behavioral strategies may not actually be revealed as an obvious change by the mentee until much later in the mentoring relationship.

OPEN-ENDED QUESTIONS

Those problems that are perceived and presented as real and immediate issues by the mentee—whether of fact or emotion—should be addressed reasonably early in the relationship. The mentor's overall purpose will be to engage the mentee in dialogue that pertains to present concerns by carefully phrasing questions to elicit a maximum of available information.

Although interacting with clearly hyper-sensitive mentee could result in an initially fragile interpersonal situation, the skilled mentor can generally better manage the evolving relationship by using language that opens rather than closes the potential for relevant facts to emerge and meaningful dialogue to occur. Certain language choices, for instance, especially when framed as part of questions, often will produce a predictably constricted reaction in a mentee. Words as innocently appearing as *What?* and especially *Why?* at the start of even a well-meaning question can be easily interpreted by a mentee as containing an accusatory message, especially in the context of other nonverbal indicators of disapproval, such as somewhat stern voice tone and eye contact (Devito, 1990; Weaver, 1993).

A mentor in education or in the workplace, for example, could make the following rather straightforward comment to a mentee: "*Why* didn't you just approach the instructor/manager at the time, or go to the person's office to ask for help?" While the mentor's point is clear, and such information will probably be necessary at some point for a meaningful discussion, nonetheless, many mentees would react as if they had to defend their decisions and actions, because the word *Why?* generally conveys the impression of a prosecutor interrogating a witness.

Add any other nonverbal behavior which signals disapproval and the odds of a predictable, almost instant negative mentee reaction are greatly increased. While not all mentees will respond quite this way, in opening up a discussion, the mentor should usually phrase questions aimed at widening rather than narrowing the avenues of conversation. The less any mentee is placed in the position of having to almost apologize for decisions and actions, the more likely will be the mutual opportunity for a genuine review of the significant facts about (and issues underlying) important events.

Questions which begin with words such as *When?*, *How?*, *Who?*, and even *What?* (as in "What happened then?") are more likely to produce an open-ended and more detailed response, and thereby encourage the mentee to reveal relevant information rather than engage in unproductive ego-defensive behavior. A mentor, for example, could ask (in a calm and concerned manner): "*What* was your reason for not approaching the instructor/manager at the time, or not going afterwards to the person's office to ask for help? Also, *what* are you planning to do if this problem continues?" These less accusatory approaches, especially when the mentor allows the mentee the time to adequately explain the situation, should create a more comfortable climate for the mentee to reflect on and examine the implications of individual decisions and actions.

DESCRIPTIVE FEEDBACK

The language, timing, and subjects addressed by the mentor in response to the mentee can clearly exert a powerful influence on the quality of the relationship. The mentor should distinguish between comments directed at the mentee's specific actions and those which attempt to uncover—by inference—motives which explain that behavior. Speculative responses which attempt to identify and explain possible motives behind mentee behaviors generally provide little constructive assistance because such a mind-reader approach is essentially assumptions-based and therefore often incorrect.

The mentor will need to be alert to this gray area of mentoring interaction. It can present more of a problem than the issue of stereotyping the mentee based on attributing the "what?" of observable behavior to the "why?" of internal motive. A mentee also could understandably resent an unsolicited intrusion into what appears to be the domain of therapeutic probing rather than that of more educationally based dialogue, in which the mentor would address more external performance related issues.

Moreover, a mentee may not be emotionally prepared to explore the interior world of personal motive, a mentor may not be professionally trained or skilled enough to really assist, and if any psychic landmines such as volatile repressed anger and unresolved conflict are stepped on in the exploration, the mentor and mentee could both find the experience very counterproductive. A mentor may unthinkingly perceive certain motives to be the internal pressure behind mentee behavior only to discover that the analysis was not only completely wrong but also now has created additional problems because of the mentor's own unjustified comments or actions based on the inaccurate attributions.

The mentor will usually be most productive if an observations-specific approach is employed with the mentee, especially in the relationship emphasis phase. If the mentee does volunteer to examine issues best referred to a counselor or other helping professional in the psychological field, the mentor can certainly offer to refer, and explain the rationale as well, so that the mentee understands the legitimate concerns and boundaries of the mentor.

Certainly, the mentee will offer self-reports of problems, strategies, and actual events not directly witnessed by the mentor. But the purpose of the mentor's early verbal comments is to assist the mentee in *gradually* illuminating areas of understanding through sensitive low-intensity questions. An overly bright spotlight of opinion, however intellectually on the mark, might also prove to be too threatening for the mentee to accept and benefit from at that stage of interaction. Descriptive words, if chosen with care, can be used to communicate a particular mentee behavior as personally experienced by the mentor. This type of mentee portrait, based on verbal feedback, can be a valuable reference point because it depends less on mentee self-reports and much more on direct mentor observation of and response to the mentee based on their mutual interaction.

A relatively mature mentee might be able to progress much faster through the learning process without appearing particularly threatened by more direct mentor feedback. As a result, a mentor might sometimes feel less compelled to express overtly respectful behaviour in an early dialogue of disagreement. However, the mentor should remember the general importance for most mentees of

experiencing openly supportive mentor behaviour in the relationship emphasis phase. By demonstrating this type of positive interactive style, the mentor can also use the approach to increase the
mentee's understanding about the interpersonal behaviors necessary for real-world acceptance of differences, negotiation, and mutual problem solving (Fisher & Ury, 1981; Jandt, 1985).

In offering descriptive verbal responses to the mentee, the
mentor can utilize some of the widely accepted techniques employed by professionals in the psychological sciences to communicate their concerns to clients. In adapting these approaches—the
"I" message, restatement, and perception check—the mentor should
view them as methods for maintaining a dialogue which has the
clear objective of offering assistance to the adult learner (Devito,
1990; Weaver, 1993). This is in no way meant to suggest a manipulative attitude. On the contrary, the mentor is attempting to
ensure that good intentions are actually translated into effective
mentoring behaviors.

The "I Am Personally Concerned" Message

When the mentor must express a concern to the mentee that
might be interpreted as critically harsh or nonaccepting, the "I"
message can minimize the potential for defensive reactions often
created by this type of direct feedback. Using this approach, the
mentor clearly assumes responsibility for being the one with the
expressed concern, thus the pronoun "I" is often used to start
the message. Although the mentor explicitly identifies a specific
problem, the underlying assumption is that even if the mentee
does not perceive or agree that a problem exists between them, if
the mentor clearly does, then both parties still have a problem. In
addition, the topic under discussion can relate to a range of substantive learning concerns, including such mentee issues as intellectual strategies and decisions, educational and/or career related
performance, behavioral actions (toward the mentor or others),
and emotional responses to stress and change.

Although the relevance and accuracy of a comment, the timing, and the overall feedback behavior may all be handled well by

the mentor, some mentees may still interpret the information as more of a personal criticism of self and less as a compliment about human potential. In such a situation, the mentor may sometimes be viewed as offering useful insight into what the mentee might become, but with a too critical focus (as interpreted by the mentee) on what the mentee has yet to achieve.

Mentees generally will benefit as adult learners from listening to and seriously considering the assessments of mentors. However, the mentor may sometimes believe that the mentee is experiencing the mentoring session more as an occasion tilted toward negative personal criticism and less as an opportunity to receive the balanced feedback of the serious critique. In this case, the mentor may need to openly inquire about the mentee's interpretations of and reactions to the critique, offer reassurance, and also connect the positive relevance of the information to the mentee's capabilities, proficiencies, goals, and recommended options for continued learning.

A mentor should be prepared to accept, as entirely understandable, a mentee's sometimes overreactive response of immediately hearing only the negative but not the positive in the feedback, especially if the mentee is insecure and requires a great deal of reassurance. In our society, many people, even the reasonably secure, still initially associate a critique offered to them—even when it overtly includes statements about positive intent and belief in their talents—with the identification of some internalized deficiency within themselves rather than the sincere assessment by others of their presumed talent.

Given the rather typical history of anger and harsh judgment which has been packaged and offered as constructive criticism in the larger society, the mentee would not need to be particularly oversensitive to personally and quickly interpret any subsequent critique as associated with a negative rather than a positive experience, and thus with anxiety-producing doubts and emotions. Obviously, it is therefore important for the mentor to remain calm and reassuring and to allow the mentee to express reasonable defensive behavior within the empathetic environment of the mentoring session.

Mentoring is learning. Mentee actions that occur outside the mentoring sessions are important, but so are the reactions to the mentor within the sessions. Mentees will have the opportunity, by working through the give and take interpersonal dialogue of the mentoring relationship, of learning to better handle challenges to their ideas and beliefs, as well as to experience the positive growth associated with the genuinely constructive critique. For some mentees, this experience will provide them with a valuable model of adult interaction. The "I" message technique, because of its unique effect, may assist them in relying less on inappropriate defensive responses as they learn more effective interpersonal skills.

The verbal content of the "I" message is designed to address four distinct yet clearly connected areas of mentor concern:

1. The actual mentee behavior which the mentor views as a problem

2. The specific examples of the objectionable and unproductive mentee behavior

3. The mentor's own negative affective (emotional) response to the particular mentee behavior which is openly identified and challenged

4. The probable counterproductive consequences of that continuing behavior on general mentee learning, and especially on the mentoring relationship if the problem behavior is occurring *between* the mentor and the mentee

Of course, the mentor does not always have to include all of these issues in a single "I" message. In fact, the mentor's emotional reaction (which will probably be expressed by words which communicate different degrees of honest concern, such as "annoyed about or by," "bothered by," "frustrated about," and even "offended at or by") might be offered later in the interaction to reduce the chances of initially overloading the message.

As an example, a mentor could employ all of the components of the "I" message technique with a mentee who has been using biased or accusatory language:

1. Identify the actual behavior. "I'm having a problem with your use of stereotyping labels."

2. Provide specific examples of the particular objectionable terms. "I hear you negatively referring to others or to me as typical left-wing, ivory tower liberals, or as the usual corporate/ government types."

3. Identify the emotional response which is creating genuine personal discomfort. "I am bothered by, or annoyed by, such labeling."

4. Clarify the consequences of continued unacceptable or inappropriate mentee behavior. "I am therefore having a difficult time in concentrating my attention on helping you, and may not continue to to do so as long as what I consider to be disrespectful or inappropriate behaviors continue to interfere with our discussions."

While overtly disruptive mentee remarks may not be that common within the mentoring relationship, if indicated, the mentor should unmistakably communicate to the mentee that mentors are not punching bags for the mentee's pent-up emotions or prejudices. The mentor can also appropriately use, for example, an "I" message to confront a mentee regarding missed mentoring sessions or tasks the mentee has agreed to fulfill but has shown no incentive to complete. In such instances, the mentor can use this technique to first directly communicate to the mentee an "I am very concerned about this particular behavior" statement, and to then to select for the remainder of the message any other points that need to be verbalized. In such instances, the mentor may have no strongly personal emotional response (such as being offended) other than clear disappointment at the mentee's lack of responsiveness.

In modeling the "I" message approach, the mentor should always attempt to demonstrate that there is a reasonable and mature means of expressing concern to another person which is not meant to be an attack, threat, or ultimatum, but rather a necessary source of information if both parties are to express their legitimate emotional reactions, as well as to rationally explore ideas about possible resolutions. Certainly, the mentor can be a significant model for the mentee of the fundamental importance, as revealed by such interpersonal demonstrations, of engaging in mature dialogue.

If the real issue is an unacceptable mentee behavior directed *at the mentor*, then, of course, this needs to be addressed immediately as the primary concern. Here the mentor will essentially be in an openly confrontive position in the attempt to point out the discrepancy between inappropriate and appropriate mentee behavior. While any of the four "I" message content areas verbalized by the mentor could provoke a defensive mentee reaction, the mentor's reference to particular mentee behaviors as an issue for the mentor *personally* could initially trigger very negative mentee feelings and actions. The mentee is likely to react much more defensively to specific one-to-one feedback interpreted as personally unacceptable by the mentor within the mentoring relationship than to, for instance, the mentor's view of how the mentee arrived at a decision or treated another person outside of their relationship.

Restatement

This technique, which is also labeled as "paraphrase" or as a component of "active or reflective listening," is a useful interpersonal communications approach for ensuring that a verbal message transmitted by the mentee (the sender) has been fully understood by the mentor (the receiver). The primary purpose of restatement is to capture the essential *informational meaning* of the intended message by restating or summarizing the key points (ideas, opinions, facts), rather than simply parroting a word-for-word playback. In using this technique, the mentor is in essence slowing down the speed of the interaction by selectively "feeding back" (to the mentee) the literal cognitive content of the mentee's message.

The mentor, without trying to extend beyond the message by adding interpretive meaning or assuming what was implied, directly asks the mentee if the verbalized summary was a factually accurate (and possibly even more specific) rendition of the mentee's original message. The mentee can then indicate that it was, or if necessary, further clarify the topic under discussion. Of course, the mentor can also reverse this process, and ask the mentee to restate the essence of the mentor's own content-focused point to ensure that the mentee has understood the essential message.

The restatement approach offers numerous advantages when utilized properly. It requires the mentor to interact with the mentee to ensure that the intended message was received—did the mentor really understand the point?—and often even assists the mentee in recognizing when a message was not clearly expressed, adequately explained, or based on a reasoned approach. The very act of restatement also behaviorally communicates and reinforces the genuine concern the mentor has for truly understanding the mentee as a significant person whose shared thinking is important.

PERCEPTION CHECKS

While restatement focuses on the factual or content dimension of the message, the perception check attempts to ensure that the underlying *emotional* component of the message is also understood. The assumption behind the technique is that personal feelings are not always openly expressed or clearly acknowledged; therefore, how a mentee actually views an issue, idea, attitude, or opinion may be misinterpreted by or not readily apparent to a mentor. A mentee's emotional position on an issue can be clarified by a direct inquiry. In specific, the mentor selects a word reflective of the emotion which appears to accurately describe the mentee's currently observable behavior (at least to the mentor).

The typical perception check thus would carefully focus on identifying an important emotional response or feeling state which either has not been verbally expressed or has been indirectly expressed to the mentor. The purpose of the method is to uncover the particular emotion that appears to be influencing or blocking the mentee's decisions or actions, but that the mentee is apparently unable to directly acknowledge as an emotional issue of relevance. The mentor, for example, can use the basic perception check technique as follows: "I am concerned about the (name the emotional state which seems most precise) feeling of dejection or lack of hope you appear to have regarding this problem."

The mentor's objective is, of course, to offer support and to help the mentee surface and openly discuss difficult-to-express feelings. By indicating that the mentee's emotional situation is often observable to others—that it is not a secret—and to clearly suggest that because the affective responses of individuals usually (and normally) influence their thinking, judgment, and behavior, the mentor can help legitimize the mature exchange of emotional reactions relevant to the exploration of issues within the mentoring relationship.

If the mentee's verbal and nonverbal behavioral responses imply a strong emotional base, but the mentee appears reluctant to openly discuss being affected by such feelings as discomfort, frustration, resentment, anger, or fear, the mentor can also carefully encourage the mentee through the perception check to deal with these reactions as a necessary part of understanding and resolving the problems under discussion. This approach is particularly important because the mentee will then be able to explore negative emotional responses such as fear of failure in the nonjudgmental context of the mentoring relationship, and thus learn to interpret personal anxiety as a controllable and not automatically self-disqualifying reaction to new and different challenges.

The objective of the mentor is to reasonably shepherd the mentee through anxiety-producing decisions and experiences so that appropriate risk-taking actions are developed as solution-focused adaptive behaviors, especially if there has been some history of lack of academic or career success. Ideally, the mentee will learn to view anxiety as a necessary and prudent "be careful" signal and not as a permanent "do not enter" sign.

The mentor who pursues this dimension of the mentoring relationship is not being cast in the role of self-appointed therapist. Instead, if meaningful growth is to occur, a legitimate component of the mentoring experience will usually require that the mentee pursue projects that are understandably perceived as anxiety-producing. Involuntary as well as voluntary engagement in the reality of change will often place the mentee in the position of confronting two central themes of adulthood—issues of control and competency.

By encouraging mentees to respond to changes which impact on their personal, academic, or career options, mentors may often involve mentees in examining personal defenses erected long ago to avoid risk of failure. The mentors' attempt to nudge mentees into action can offer a healthy opportunity for mentees to examine their own self-limiting behaviors. But mentors should remember that the often intense need for ego safety required to explore uncharted developmental terrain can be difficult even for the self-assured and independent mentee, much less for the unsure mentee with low self-esteem.

Also, the issue of competency often surfaces when the mentee must evaluate the variety of new proficiencies required to survive in a changed environment. The dynamics of significant change force the mentee to inventory those personal competencies that have already been developed, to anticipate which career-related knowledge and skills relied on before may now be obsolete or even dysfunctional, and to predict the education, training, experience, and credentials essential for future mobility. This particular supportive facet of the mentor role has great importance because a major premise of the mentoring model of development is that the mentor will be "accompanying" the mentee through actual decision-making and task performance situations by being a *psychological and emotional resource* as well as an intellectual guide.

Often, the perception check is the correct technique for the mentor to employ when powerful but misdirected or unacknowledged emotions appear to be driving a mentee to engage in behaviors that are viewed as less than self-enlightened. It is appropriate when personal insight into the emotional forces propelling a mentee's actions might offer the clarification required for meaningful problem solving. This type of verbal check also helps ensure that the mentee's message has been reasonably well-examined, understood cognitively, and processed emotionally by the mentor.

NONJUDGMENTAL RESPONSES

As a general approach, the mentor will often elicit a more comprehensive explanation from the mentee if the mentor's own initial verbal and nonverbal responses do not actively indicate either approval or disapproval but instead communicate a concerned attempt to comprehend the ideas, feelings, and experiences as presented from the mentee's point of view. The mentor's more experienced approach may allow the mentor to arrive at a conclusion well before the mentee believes there has been a reasonable examination of the facts. If the mentor immediately suggests either agreement or disagreement based on limited information, the mentee may misinterpret this as a trivialization of the mentee's issues because such mentor behaviors are perceived as a lack of interest or willingness to engage in mutual dialogue.

The mentor's expression of emotional and psychological support for the mentee's continuing development as an adult learner is, of course, always beneficial. But the mentor must be careful about expressing heavy-handed pro or con judgments about the mentee's particular ideas, beliefs, or actions. The word judgment usually indicates that one has openly taken a favorable or unfavorable position on a topic, issue, or behavior, and thus implies that a particular correct or incorrect attitude is embedded in the viewpoint. Ideally, the interpersonal conditions of the relationship will provide an opportunity for learning and growth through the dialogue experience of mentoring. The mentee will thereby become accustomed to analytically examining rather than merely defending decisions about issues or actions as a healthy, mature part of adult mentor-mentee interaction. The nonjudgmental atmosphere of the mentoring relationship appears to develop this special type of potential and to foster the self-assessment and critical reflection which needs to be practiced as an adult behavior.

This nonjudgmental approach, however, is not meant to suggest a value, or position-neutral, response by the mentor to mentoring interaction. On the contrary, the mentor may need to openly confront the mentee's approaches and strategies out of concern for the individual's overall development. The mentor, of course, must distinguish between *differences of opinion* which involve another adult's legitimate right (even as the learner) to finally arrive at an entirely different cognitive position and the *process* of engaging in valid educational confrontation for the purpose of assisting and enhancing the personal, academic, or career potential of the mentee as an adult learner. Usually, the mentor will be reviewing and if necessary challenging the mentee's strategies for decision making rather than commenting on actual mentee actions, unless specific behaviors are clearly identified as counterproductive, such as frequent and inappropriate avoidant or aggressive responses.

An important reason for the mentor to assume a nonjudgmental posture will be to assist the mentee in developing proficiency in the dialogue of interpersonal interaction and to recognize the importance of respectful discussion as a problem-solving and decision-making activity without the precondition, requirement, or expectation of mutual agreement. Even polite disagreement with a mentee's views may sometimes be interpreted as *de facto* disrespect, especially if the mentee lacks adequate information and experience (at whatever age) to realize that not all opinions are based on informed understanding. The mentor, in fact, may need to preface some remarks with an explanation that highlights the positive learning goals of the mentor-mentee interaction. The art of the mentor will be to transform even the act of constructive confrontation into a meaningful learning experience for the mentee.

SUMMARY

The definition, purpose, and specific mentor verbal and non-verbal behaviors of the relationship emphasis function are presented in Figure 3.1. The essential quality associated with this dimension of mentoring is *trust*, which is considered fundamental to the development of a successful mentoring relationship. The guidelines covered in this chapter assume an active participation by the mentor to ensure that the early and vital relational connection is made with the mentee. Also, the impact of this particular mentor function is intensified because it forms the initial impression on the mentee about the mentor as a professional as well as the expectations of the potential value of the mentoring experience.

Relationship Emphasis

Conveys through active, empathetic listening a genuine understanding and acceptance of the mentees' feelings

Purpose

To create a psychological climate of trust which allows mentees to
honestly share and reflect upon their personal experiences (positive
and negative) as adult learners

Mentor Behaviors:

* Practice responsive listening (verbal and nonverbal reactions that
  signal sincere interest).
* Ask open-ended questions related to expressed immediate concerns about actual situations.
* Provide descriptive feedback based on observations rather than inferences of motives.
* Use perception checks to ensure comprehension of feelings.
* Offer nonjudgmental sensitive responses to assist in clarification of
  emotional states and reactions.

Figure 3.1 Summary of relationship emphasis function of the mentor
role.

CHAPTER 4

Expanding the Informational Base

A significant component of mentoring will involve mentor-mentee interaction based on shared information. The use of facts in a mentoring relationship, of course, involves a clear emphasis on the mentee as the beneficiary. Together, the following two approaches to framing questions should produce a reasonable informational profile of the mentee and thereby enable the mentor to better understand and address the needs of each individual as a unique adult learner:

1. To obtain relevant *facts about the mentee's purpose* for entering into a mentoring relationship, the mentor should employ questions that reveal several types of basic information: what are the mentee's personal, educational, and career plans, and what is the mentee's current situation relative to achieving any stated goals?

2. To obtain significant *facts about what the mentee actually knows* relevant to the world of educational, training, and career options, the mentor should pose questions that uncover the basis for mentee beliefs: what concrete information does the mentee possess, and what are the sources of this knowledge?

Using a factual approach to problem solving may appear self-evident to a mentor. The mentee, however, may not always be experienced enough to evaluate if *relevant* data has been acquired to constitute a substantive starting point for personal, educational, and career decision making. The mentor, for example, will need to guard against relying on the impression that a mentee who appears certain about career choice has actually based the decision on a factually accurate and realistic assessment. Although a mentee may initially prefer to engage in only general discussion about important issues and concerns, the mentor should be careful to recognize that continued lack of reasonable self-disclosure or ability to discuss details may actually indicate that the mentee has not yet obtained sufficient and reliable informational reference points.

The mentor, while engaging in information emphasis behaviors, will therefore often need to *directly* request detailed explanations from the mentee to ensure that the advice offered is based on reasonably specific knowledge about the individual adult learner. The mentor cannot simply operate on the assumption that a mentee has already obtained an adequate amount of pragmatic information to formulate realistic and attainable goals or to pursue educational and career decisions. By a skillful use of probing questions within the evolving dialogue, the mentor will be more factually prepared to tailor advice to the specific needs of the particular mentee.

The following six behaviors will usually enable the mentor to better understand the mentee and thus promote a realistic discussion of plans and progress:

1. Ask questions aimed at a factual assessment of the current situation.

2. Review relevant background to develop an adequate profile.

3. Ask probing questions which require concrete answers.

4. Offer directive-type comments about present problems and solutions.

5. Make restatements to ensure factual and interpretive clarity.

6. Rely on facts as an integral component of the dialogue of mentoring interaction.

The cumulative objective of these behaviors will be to create a factual foundation upon which the mentor and mentee can together plan and evaluate mentee-specific progress toward goals. Such approaches, which will now be separately examined, can be used at any point in a mentoring session, especially when *what* a mentee wants, or knows, needs to be clarified.

QUESTIONS TO DETERMINE
CURRENT SITUATION

To establish a reasonable profile of a mentee, the mentor will often need to rely on questions aimed at assuring factual understanding of the mentee's *present* educational and career situation. Sometimes a mentee will volunteer information almost immediately and also be relatively well informed about career or academic concerns. Sometimes, however, a mentee will appear knowledgeable because of the ability to use the correct terminology of education or the workplace, but have little more than very basic information obtained from college catalogues, workplace and career articles and pamphlets, or acquaintances.

A mentee in an educational context, for example, may not only express interest in becoming a therapist because of a fascination with human behavior courses, but also base such an early career decision primarily on personal experience as a paraprofessional, or even as a patient, in a community-based therapy program designed to assist persons with alcohol or drug addictions. Such a history may explain the clear motivation behind the mentee's career choice. The mentor can also assume that the mentee will have access to professionals in the mental health–social service field as part of participation in an actual degree program, and subsequently will gain more specific insight into the realities of the chosen field. However, the mentor can still directly pose questions aimed at revealing the mentee's current knowledge about the relationship between academic degrees, professional interests, and career opportunities. The mentee may not have examined the options available to those with two- or four-year degrees, or advanced training, or really understand that the word *therapist* is an umbrella term which covers a variety of specialities, from social work interventions with dysfunctional families, to counseling adolescents with drug problems, to working with parents convicted of child abuse.

A mentee already in the workplace may be considering combining the pursuit of a college degree with full-time employment. The mentor can assist by inquiring as to the mentee's present decisions and actions with respect to balancing work and part-time study. Questions can focus on basic factual realities: Has the immediate supervisor been informed to prevent possible future scheduling issues, such as work-related mandatory overtime or anticipated training obligations? The mentor can also ask a range of other questions: Has the mentee determined if tuition costs, etc., will be covered by the organization, examined the feasibility of receiving academic credit for work-experience, or investigated the market value of the degree which is being pursued?

The mentor's ability and experience help to *interpret* information for the mentee, as well as to refer the mentee to reliable and current sources, such as other professionals or experts in particular academic and career fields. Here the mentor can play a key role in helping a mentee *translate facts into decisions*. Of course, to offer meaningful assistance will require that the mentor has a genuine sense of the present needs, interests, and plans of the particular mentee seated across the desk, not just of mentees in general.

The mentor will therefore need to direct rather specific questions at the mentee's current and projected situation regarding such real-world issues as:

1. The time available for training, courses, and follow-up study outside of class or work

2. The completion status (actual or anticipated) with respect to the prerequisites needed to even apply for some educational programs or career tracks

3. The mentee's actual ability to manage financial responsibilities in considering or continuing full-time (if applicable) study to obtain the desired degree or certification credentials

Possible problems associated with the overall logistics of committing to both work and a long-term academic or training program will also need to be identified, especially with regard to the realistic availability of family or community resources the mentee may ing on to assist with such concerns as transportation, child care, and economic assistance.

QUESTIONS ABOUT MENTEE BACKGROUND

The mentor should be prepared to discuss aspects of the mentee's background which are related to the topics appropriate for a mentoring session, such as issues centered on educational, training, and career progress. However, the mentor should be careful about probing into inappropriate aspects of the mentee's life experience, such as highly personal concerns regarding problems in childhood, sexual functioning, or substance abuse, which the mentee may even raise and connect with current life events. Any encouragement by the mentor that the mentee should reveal in-depth details, and that they will then mutually explore the significance of such difficult experiences, could clearly involve crossing the sometimes thin but important line between educator/manager and counselor or therapist.

In actuality, a mentor may need to respond to immediate mentee self-disclosure regarding serious personal issues, which may have created emotional or psychological problems that are negatively contributing to academic or career performance, by referring the mentee to a professional with the expertise to offer (if necessary) a meaningful therapeutic intervention.

For example, if the mentee raises concerns about such present problems as persistent inability to sleep, concentrate, or complete assignments, the mentor should consider an initial referral—to college counselors in education or to workplace personnel specialists who are usually located in government and business human resource offices. The mentee in this situation, of course, may not directly and openly state that a personal problem exists, but dwell on the consequences instead, such as receiving low grades due to an inability to concentrate on an exam, or always falling behind with reading and papers, or erratic attendance at class. The mentor can also focus on supporting the practical performance concerns as well, and encourage the mentee to seek assistance not necessarily as a matter of therapy, but rather as a pragmatic immediate issue of avoiding a permanent "F" on a college transcript.

In the workplace, the mentor can apply the same focus by supporting the mentee's effort to function at the highest level of competency which the mentee believes is possible. If the mentor can establish, through questions, that particular problems have occurred before or are part of the mentee's pattern of behavior, the mentor can also indicate that perhaps there are important issues to be explored that may continue to impact on performance if left unresolved. In fact, the mentor can suggest to a reluctant mentee that other professionals (beside the mentor) may help the mentee to find workable solutions, and that seeking such assistance would be a mature decision by any adult suffering from a negative impact on the quality of personal and professional life.

PROBING QUESTIONS

A probing question should not be equated with a particularly rigorous behavioral style of eliciting information. Instead, the function of a probe is to engage the mentee in an open dialogue. Questions which require only generic or yes/no responses have usually been inadvertently phrased so that they essentially limit or close off the number of mentee options for a meaningful answer. Questions designed as probes often begin with words such as *when, where, what,* and *how*. The mentor's objective—much like a journalist pursuing facts—is to collect specific information. However, the mentor must be careful to communicate such questions within the context of a respectful mentoring and not a hard-nosed news-gathering session.

The mentor, for instance, could probe into a mentee's reasons for asserting a strong preference or aversion to a topic or career by posing such questions as: "Would you give me some examples from your own experience?" or "What happened to you personally?" The mentor's objective is to encourage the mentee to expand the factual information base available for use within the mentoring relationship by focusing on concrete facts, perceptions, and events rather than generalized, vague, or dead-end yes/no explanations.

Using this approach, the mentor should then be able to form a reasonably substantive portrait of each unique mentee and therefore engage in more relevant dialogue.

If the mentee appears uncomfortable with any of these direct questions, the mentor should certainly explain that the purpose of such probes is to better understand the mentee as a person, but that if any question is too personal, the mentee always has the right to so inform the mentor, who will respect the mentee's preferences not to inquire about certain topics.

DIRECTIVE-TYPE QUESTIONS

The exploratory and options-centered indirect mentor approach that is characteristic of much mentor-mentee dialogue is clearly appropriate for a substantial amount of the evolving mentoring interaction. Certainly, the mentor will be using the interpersonal dynamics of mentoring as an opportunity for the mentee to assume the responsibility for decisions and actions as an independent adult learner.

However, an important aspect of the mentoring relationship will also involve the mentor's directive-style comments about present mentee problems and solutions. A mentor should consider providing direct instructions as to particular actions the mentee should definitely follow if, for instance, a situation occurs in which a serious event is imminent. In school this might be failing a course because of not contacting an instructor about missed classes and assignments or not filling out withdrawal forms for a class and receiving an "F" instead of a "W." In the workplace the mentee might be facing a marginal performance appraisal because of not responding to a supervisor's offer to meet and discuss problems, expressing inappropriate behavior with a supervisor or other employees, or blaming others for negative consequences, such as poor evaluations.

In attempting to contain the negative consequences caused by immediate and significant problems, the mentor directly intervenes by stating an action the mentee should follow to resolve the present situation. This more prescriptive behavioral role of a mentor could be necessary if the mentee is inexperienced or naive about pursuing any still available options. However, this overly involved approach is not without risk. A mentor, by assuming this more proactive interventionist role, could also encourage mentee dependency while primarily attempting to assist the mentee in regaining stability and directly surviving the current problem.

In general, however, the "no pain, no gain" approach to human development, which some mentors might *too rigidly* follow, could clearly be unproductive in a mentoring relationship because it could diminish the legitimate role of the mentor as a guide through some of the perils of the mentee's journey. Certainly, an individual can profit from painful experiences. For example, the lesson that one can survive academic or career disappointment, unfairness, and initial lack of success, but still continue forward, is an extremely important lesson to be learned. And, in fact, much valuable learning derives from the experience of direct, personal, and normal frustration and struggle which is inherent in the process of developing mature problem-solving and decision-making skills.

A major purpose of mentoring, though, is to maximize positive learning, not by simply and inappropriately shielding the mentee, but by reducing the appropriately *preventable* negative cost of trial-and-error learning. Mentor judgment, of course, will be required to ascertain if the mentee is repeating a pattern of dependency behavior by reenacting a relationship of emergencies. A direct intervention, therefore, should be viewed as a legitimate means that enables the mentee to continue learning, while the mentor monitors the journey as a type of damage control specialist. The mentor can always consider referral to a helping professional if the underlying issues driving the mentee into continued unproductive strategies or behaviors appear beyond the scope of a mentoring session.

The distinction between indirect and direct influence should be a significant concern for a mentor. A simplified but useful guideline when dealing with a mentee facing a very serious threat would be the analogy to a drowning person overwhelmed by the event itself (Schlossberg, 1989). There may be current decisions to be made (deadlines, extensions, untapped requests for help) which could reduce the negative consequences of poor strategies and inaction. The mentor could then immediately throw the life preserver of intervention (including follow-up) over the mentee by overtly offering direct actions for the mentee to pursue or by taking actions on the mentee's behalf, such as making telephone calls and personal inquiries.

This approach can communicate to the mentee that the mentor—as a concerned person who represents the organization— cares enough to directly offer immediate rational guidance and emotional support. A well-intentioned mentor whose noninvolvement comments and lack of action imply that "almost drowning" will somehow prove to be a valuable learning experience could face the reality of eroded credibility. The mentee could easily interpret the mentor's attitude as patronizing and condescending. The mentor, therefore, will need to decide if a more or less interventionist role is required based on the mentee's current problem, rather than to rely on the inaccurate simplicity of a predetermined and then imposed "no pain, no gain" approach. The mentor's attention should be centered on the essential issue of deciding what blend of learning from experience will best serve mentee development.

Of course, the available and most appropriate options are not always crystal clear. However, to continue the analogy, a mentor in doubt can generally rely on the life preserver of directive comments. Especially early in the relationship, this is an effective strategy to keep the mentee afloat while the mentoring relationship helps the mentee work on "swimming lessons." To watch the mentee disappear beneath the waves and then attempt a later rescue if the mentee does indeed almost "drown" can have an effect opposite to that of genuinely positive mentoring. It may, in fact, reinforce the all too frequent negative experience of trial-and-error learning as failure. Direct instructions provide the advantage of legitimate mentor assistance built into the self-correction component to minimize any of the preventable ego-destructive cost associated with mentee learning.

The last experience most mentees need more of, especially those with a history of failure, is additional failure. The mentor, as an experienced professional, generally instructs with the objec-

tive of assisting while challenging the mentee to achieve the legitimate confidence that derives from learned and performance-based
competency. Sometimes this instruction needs to tilt toward more
directive-type comments deliberately aimed at eliciting immediate
mentee actions to resolve pressing problems..

RESTATEMENTS: FACTUAL AND
INTERPRETIVE ACCURACY

A mentor will need to be concerned about assessing not only
the extent of the mentee's knowledge but also the interpretation of
the collected facts. A mentee could have correct and current information but still misunderstand the relevance of the facts as they
apply to individual educational and career options. An exploration of the information base of mentoring, therefore, should include a review aimed at determining comprehension of the facts
from the mentee's point of view. This approach will also help to
accomplish a critical task of the mentoring relationship: to *center*
the mentor's advice and guidance on information specific to the
mentee's options, goals, and choices.

A mentor can use the restatement technique to ensure clarity
of understanding by directly paraphrasing statements made by the
mentee. The intention is to feed back the mentee's factual content
as rephrased and even interpreted by the mentor, but not in the
form of a simplistic and possibly irritating tape recording. The
mentor, for example, can summarize the essential points expressed
in a rather detailed explanation offered by the mentee regarding a course, degree, training, or career choice by stating: "If I've
understood the main issue, you're reluctant to take another Span-
ish course because you are certain that you'll have another bad
experience with any instructor from that department," or "So the
bottom line, from what you're saying, is that you are convinced
that your supervisor is hypercritical about your performance, and
nothing you can do will really change that situation, except a
transfer."

In restating the mentee's verbal message, the mentor thus attempts to ascertain *what the mentee knows and believes*. During this process, the mentor also helps the mentee to clarify general ideas and thereby arrive at more detail-oriented and realistic decisions. The restatement component of the information emphasis function therefore achieves three valuable tasks:

1. It allows the mentor to provide feedback to the mentee based on the mentee's own perceptions and statements.

2. It enables the mentor to more precisely determine if the mentee's responses are anchored in a realistic appraisal of the actual situation.

3. It provides a more definite factual base from which the mentor can draw in offering the mentee particular advice.

FACT FINDING AS AN INTEGRAL COMPONENT

In posing questions that attempt to reveal each mentee's unique needs, experiences, and goals, the mentor's primary objective is to generate specific information which can be used as a guide for planning. However, the mentor should avoid a stilted style of questioning that excessively uses the restatement technique and thereby too often belabors the obvious regarding points that are already clearly understood by both parties. The mentor should also avoid a too rapid-fire and essentially overbearing approach. If the mentor cuts off the mentee as soon as a fact is revealed, and then poses another question, such an approach could produce a staccato effect and thus create the impression of a one-way grilling session instead of a mentoring dialogue.

Mentees usually need to learn how to apply information to their individual issues and objectives and not just how to acquire it. Mentors should recognize that even those mentees who are proficient at obtaining data may still require considerable assistance in interpreting the actual value of facts to them as adult learners faced with educational and career decisions.

SUMMARY

By attempting to collect as much information as possible about the mentee, the mentor is essentially speeding up the natural process of getting to know someone which would occur in more casual conversation. In fact, the mentor and the mentee may not be together often enough for the mentor to accumulate an adequate informational profile of the mentee if specific questions are not part of the mentoring dialogue. The techniques listed in Figure 4.1 are a summary of the reasonable mentor-initiated behaviors that can assist in the expansion of the informational base within the mentoring relationship. The overall purpose is to ensure that the mentor knows the mentee well enough to offer meaningful advice.

Information Emphasis

Directly requests detailed information from and offers specific suggestions to mentees about their current plans and progress in achieving personal, educational, and career goals

Purpose

To ensure that advice offered is based on accurate and sufficient knowledge of individual mentees

Mentor Behaviors

* Ask questions aimed at assuring factual understanding of present educational and career situation.
* Review relevant background to develop adequate personal profile.
* Ask probing questions which require concrete answers.
* Offer directive-type comments about present problems and solutions that should be considered.
* Make restatements to ensure factual accuracy and interpretive understanding.
* Rely on facts as an integral component of the decision-making process.

Figure 4.1 Summary of information emphasis function of the mentor role.

CHAPTER 5

Exploring the Facilitative Dimension

The essential value of facilitation is to help mentees reflect upon and consider *alternative* points of view. In the facilitative role, the mentor focuses on guiding mentees through a more comprehensive and reasonably substantive review of currently held views regarding their education, training, career, or job situations. The primary context in which the mentoring occurs—education or employment—will also influence the particular interests, ideas, beliefs, and abilities which are examined, as well as the general paths of information to be explored.

The following six approaches to facilitation can enhance the mentor's ability to interact productively with the mentee:

1. Pose hypothetical questions to expand individual views.

2. Uncover the underlying experiential and informational basis for assumptions.

3. Present multiple viewpoints to generate a more in-depth analysis of decisions.

4. Examine the seriousness of commitment to goals.

5. Analyze reasons for current pursuits.

6. Review recreational and other vocational preferences.

HYPOTHETICAL QUESTIONS

The overall purpose of this mentor function is to provide a variety of perspectives for mentees to examine regarding their own decisions about attainable personal, academic, and work-place objectives. An explanation provided by Walter and Peller (1992) of their solutions-oriented approach to short-term or brief therapy also has relevance for the hypothetical questions component of facilitation dialogue regarding actual mentee problems:

> The hypothetical solution frame is used under these circumstances: when we have difficulty with clients coming up with a positive framing of their goal; when we seem to have difficulty with clients coming up with exceptions since they seem to be having difficulty viewing their situation in any other than the problem frame; or when we want to check how the exceptions compare with how clients imagine the solution to be. . . . Many clients respond to the hypothetical solution question with answers that describe remote solutions. Clients describe solutions that will be occurring several months or longer from now and that describe a state of being or the conclusion to a process. The answer is helpful in that it describes what they are ultimately looking for. All we want to do, however, is facilitate the clients getting on track or in process. (pp. 76, 86)

Although the mentor is not functioning as a therapist with a client, the mentor can certainly utilize the "what if" approach to promote a mature exploration of important topics. Of course, to effectively perform as a guide who poses hypothetical questions in the facilitator role, the mentor will need to rely on both the interpersonal relationship of trust and the specific informational profile of the mentee already established in the mentoring relationship. For the mentee to legitimately benefit from a facilitative experience, the mentor must therefore understand the mentee well enough to offer *informed* opinions. By connecting with the unique personality of the mentee, the mentor can thus participate in a meaningful review of previously expressed goals, raise options which might offer new insight as the mentee contemplates present and future educational and career development, and investigate possible future solutions to current problems.

To encourage an *expanded* view of educational and career opportunities, the mentor should directly introduce into the mentoring dialogue the type of questions which utilize suppositions as the basis for examining alternatives. In framing these hypothetical questions, the mentor will attempt to create a *simulated reality* for the mentee to consider as a reference point for projecting into the future. In some instances, the mentor may attempt to explore different solutions to problems about which the mentee already has a fixed view. Of course, the idea of examining other possible courses of action may not immediately appeal to a mentee who is apparently locked into previously arrived at and very definite plans. Sometimes, in fact, mentees may be very unreceptive to the pursuit of additional information outside of their proposed agendas.

The mentor in education, for example, may ask such hypothetical questions as: "I know you definitely think you'll be accepted, but if the nursing program you hope to enter doesn't accept you, what are your options at that point? And are there things you can do now just in case this happens, so you'll have a fallback position at that time?" With respect to the workplace, the mentor could pose such questions as: "I understand that you would rather only continue in computers because it's one of your real interests, where you think your talent is, and that you don't see yourself as a 'people person,' but what if the company decides to require training and evaluation of employees as members of teams? What are your plans if this happens?"

In addition, the mentor in college could also use the "what if" approach to encourage mentees to consider alternatives *beyond* their own assessment of themselves. A mentor, for example, could state to a mentee who is reluctant to pursue courses in a particular field: "I know you've said that accountancy is very competitive, *but have you really looked at your own ability* to make it as an accountant? Your overall academic record in math is excellent. And you did get an "A" in the introductory accounting course." Also, in the workplace, a mentor could suggest to mentees who are convinced that their fear of public speaking is insurmountable and is the major reason that they have not, or cannot, apply for career positions involving podium-style presentations, that: "I understand that you felt humiliated by that unfortunate experience three years ago, *but have you considered what you might accomplish with proper training*, since your knowledge of the topic clearly wasn't the problem then, and still isn't now?"

An objective of the mentor, of course, is to help assess the extent to which the mentee has established goals based on a realistic analysis and interpretation of the obtainable facts. Mentees will generally benefit from this pragmatic assistance in reviewing a variety of workable personal choices regarding educational and career-related decisions. During this exploratory process, most mentees will also profit from positive and sensitive reassurance. This is true especially if their current plans and goals require reappraisal and modification, as exemplified by the mentee considering a learning project (like the skills of oral presentations) which has been avoided, or the mentee either learning to adapt to group-centered work environments or placing employment at risk.

A mentor cannot predict the effect of such intangibles as internal motivation on mentee success, and in fact should be cautious about overtly discouraging a mentee's pursuit of what may appear to be unattainable educational and career dreams. Still the mentor should consider engaging the mentee in a concrete, real-world review based on specific facts about the following six topic areas:

1. The mentee's already mapped-out strategies to reach goals

2. Timeframes planned for achievement

3. The various requirements and credentials

4. Available personal, social, and organizational support systems

5. Past task performance

6. Personal determination to succeed as already indicated by a consistent commitment to follow through on immediate priorities

However, the mentor must also ensure that this increased emphasis on more objectively based data does not intimidate or suggest any accusatory views regarding the mentee's sincerity or motivation. In exploring the "what if" aspects, the mentor should therefore be careful to avoid communicating a lack of confidence in mentees by too aggressively attempting to pin down the facts for use as references in the mentoring dialogue. Instead, the facilitative focus dimension should be a thoughtful and balanced review of past mentee accomplishments, perceived current potential, and future plans. This review also represents a valuable opportunity to assist mentees in moving beyond unresolved difficulties in which they may have become emeshed and then stuck.

This type of mutually explored assessment is a particularly relevant approach if the issues raised for discussion by the mentees revolve around such underlying themes as what "should or might have been," with the mentee resorting to self-blame or describing the self as victim. The mentor's objective in this situation would be to help the mentee maturely examine and thereby learn from even painful and admittedly ego-deflating experiences, especially by providing a clearer focus on the extent to which the mentee may have contributed to the unsuccessful results. The overall goal should be to assist the mentee with current problems while also developing the mentee's ability to initiate more productive responses and actions if similar events should occur in the future.

Because the mentor's purpose is to carefully rely on the factual record as an important reference point, the mentor will need to openly raise concerns about events that clearly reveal mentee avoidance or lack of appropriate responsibility. However, in attempting to balance the negative and the positive, the mentor must remember not only to compliment successful results, but also to avoid superficially glossing over mentee achievements, especially with respect to realistic planning for the future. Some mentees may present a profile of talent and competency in a variety of academic or career-related areas, and may also be faced with choosing between personal preferences, values, and interests, and the sometimes rock-hard issues of livelihood. Certainly, these significant decisions require considerable self-reflection by the mentee.

The mentor should therefore explore the *facts of the dream* in a particularly sensitive and respectful manner, as well as display an honest, factual, and clear-headed interest, by engaging the mentee in the sometimes pleasant, as well as sometimes unpleasant, mature self-appraisal of tasks completed and responsibilities met, or not—and the implications for the future.

UNCOVERING ASSUMPTIONS

The mentor will usually have to carefully uncover the underlying basis for the assumptions—both experiential and informational—influencing the mentees' plans and actions. Some mentees may confidently proceed as if the operational assumptions behind their decisions were unquestionably valid. In actuality, however, they may not possess either the significant information to decide important personal choices or the sufficient experience to interpret which educational, training, and career paths to pursue.

The mentor can often act as the important reality check who examines the basis for the mentee's opinions about the topics discussed in mentoring sessions. In assessing the connection between the mentee's experiences and present beliefs, the mentor will usually have some pertinent data already supplied by the mentee. It may be necessary as well to determine how much the mentee is relying on first or second-hand reference points as the reliable basis for decisions. Moreover, the mentor will need to be alert for indications that a mentee may be generalizing from too confined a base of personal experience, especially if the mentee repeatedly offers, as the only valid source for personal decision making, references limited to the same specific events or activities.

However, the mentor should carefully approach this issue by assuring the mentee that questions and comments are neither meant to invalidate nor criticize the significance of such prior experiences. Instead, the mentor should stress that the point of an analytical exploration is to help mentees more precisely examine their facts, perceptions, and conclusions, and to ensure that they anchor the interpretation of their own experiences in the more weathered and seasoned assistance of others who can act as expert resources. A mentor may need to stress that the act of personal reflection is meant to contribute to rather than diminish from the value of the mentee's experiences as a meaningful source of learning.

When exploring the informational base, the mentor should inquire in some detail about the specific facts underlying the mentee's beliefs and decisions. A mentee may not have arrived at conclusions in a logical or systematic manner, and the mentor may discover serious omissions in the factual foundation upon which the mentee has built educational, training, and career plans. In addition, the rapidly changing demands and requirements of the contemporary and future workplace may be particularly difficult to understand or anticipate, especially if the mentee's knowledge is somewhat obsolete.

Also, a mentee may clearly express interest in improvement and success and even demonstrate sincere intentions by actively pursuing academic courses and work-related training activities, yet have very little sense of an overall plan to accomplish long-term goals. The mentor in such instances can play a significant role in helping the mentee formulate an educational or career road-map based on realistic, specific, and attainable objectives. For example, the mentor can assist the mentee in identifying and planning for the hard to predict but probable intersecting routes that will require balancing the multiple demands on personal energy, time, financial, social, and family resources. Such realities are often more difficult to objectify than the established, tangible, and formal pathways of requirements, credentials, and necessary career training and competencies that lead to future goals.

Moreover, mentors can challenge mentees to explore opportunities beyond their own initial expectations about educational and career options. Mentees, of course, may express great uncertainty regarding the individual probability of their personal success, and mentors can help them to more fully and accurately examine the blend of experience and information which has been the source of their perceptions and decisions. Some mentees, in fact, may have clearly *underestimated* or *undervalued* their potential. In such instances, the mentees could benefit from a mentor-initiated review as a means of surfacing what is often a hidden low self-esteem problem. The mentor in the facilitator role can truly practice the behavioral art of exploring the possible.

MULTIPLE VIEWPOINTS

In offering multiple views for the mentee to consider, the mentor attempts to extend the mentoring dialogue beyond the ideas and beliefs already expressed by the mentee. Rather than rely only on hypothetical or exploratory questions, the mentor offers other legitimate viewpoints that directly differ from the mentee's presently held opinions. This exposure to a variety of new perspectives can itself be an enriching growth experience for a mentee.

The mentor, for instance, may need to explain that contrary to a mentee's fixed view about being too old to attempt courses in new fields such as social service or photography, that the *facts* regarding the actual age of the participants who engage in such educational activities vary considerably from the mentee's "unsubstantiated" opinions. The mentor may also need to provide a reasonable amount of concrete information to demonstrate (to mentees of various ages) that often strongly held personal views about the ability to adapt and change are based less on the realities of chronological age and more on an individual's confidence and willingness to experiment. Also, a mentor can respond to mentees who still insist that certain career fields are essentially gender dominated, such as nursing for females or engineering for males, with facts that allow the mentee to develop a more comprehensive understanding than the mentee's current and narrow historical and cultural perspective has allowed.

Mentees can thus learn to discover other more meaningful and accurate interpretations, and therefore recognize that they may have arrived at flawed conclusions regarding their beliefs about aptitudes and careers. Some mentees, for example, may still be confused by the sociocultural constraints imposed by assumed gender-limitations in the past, and not completely comprehend the present and future options and opportunities now open to all adult learners based on talent. This approach could challenge both males and females to consider and plan alternative educational and career choices.

The multiple viewpoints approach is also aimed at generating a more in-depth review of mentee decisions. It is especially valuable when the mentee appears unable to formulate or examine other than currently expressed views because of a limited or unexamined base of experience or information. In addition, the mentor may find that the mentee's approach to understanding and resolving issues is relatively unsystematic, and that familiarity with the essentials of the critical thinking process would sharpen this ability. In this case, the mentor could introduce the mentee to the generally standard approach relied on in much rational analysis: identification of specific components of a problem, creation of feasible solutions, review of proposed options, final decision, and follow-through based on actions required to obtain results.

The mentor, for example, could suggest that a mentee conduct an initial personal study of the important differences—to the mentee—between a two-year or a four-year degree in the health or helping professions fields. Based on analyzing the issue from a number of points of view, such as career potential, financial considerations, and actual ability to realistically complete either program, the mentor and mentee could then engage in a mutual examination of the options open to the mentee. This effort will offer the mentee a significant opportunity to engage in rational analysis of a problem about which the mentee also has a vested interest.

There is, of course, some potential for legitimate disagreement when firmly held beliefs are questioned, and the mentor will need to distinguish between examining viable points of difference and overriding the mentee's right to a separate affective response and cognitive position. This is not to suggest that the dialogue be tame or watered down; the mentee will usually profit from the vigorous engagement of spirited conversation. However, the important point is not simply to challenge the mentee's current views but rather to introduce into the dialogue the reality that other views worth considering do exist. The mentor generally acts as a guide during this exploration of an educational and career landscape which will be familiar to the mentor, but often relatively uncharted terrain to the mentee.

SERIOUSNESS OF COMMITMENT

In approaching the issue of the mentees' commitment to their expressed goals, the mentor usually will have some empirical evidence, such as completion of academic courses, job training, or work-related tasks to reference as a demonstration of serious intent. Many mentees can handle the normal frustration of significant learning, enjoy the excitement of the challenge, and show a reasonably consistent pattern of achievement. A difficult problem for the mentor, however, may be that of pointing out to a mentee who is quite interested and capable of planning, but not strong on follow-through, the critical differences between stated intentions, actions, performance, and evaluation of results.

For some adult learners, identifying goals and the strategies to accomplish them may also prove to be quite different than the ongoing reality of deferring gratification of immediate pleasure and imposing the self-discipline required to complete assignments and meet strict deadlines. Some mentees may find the continuing commitment of time and energy to be much more difficult than anticipated as a daily fact of life. They may need to consider more realistic (possibly less ambitious) educational and career goals, especially if there is a considerable discrepancy between their intention and objectives and their motivation and aptitudes.

A mentor, for instance, may need to point out that the mentee's intention to review class notes at work during lunchtime, which was previously factored into the general study plan as a certain percentage of available time, appears not to have become a consistent action. In this example, the mentee has obviously not followed through on a personal commitment that now jeopardizes the actual task accomplishment of a realistic goal. Plans were not translated into operational activities. For the mentor, the area of immediate concern could include issues of mentee motivation, time management, or even underestimated fatigue, rather than only poor mentee judgment about aptitude or ability to intellectually handle the work. In fact, the problem may be explained more by inability to deal with the demands of the overall employment and study workload.

By contrast, a mentee may have worked very hard to achieve an unrealistic objective, and despite the avid pursuit of the goal, still have had little or no demonstrable success. As a result, the mentee may not have anything tangible (good grades, completion of training or degrees, promotion) which would be generally accepted by society-at-large as the observable record of serious commitment. In this case, a conscientious mentee will have devoted a great deal of time and energy to a clearly unsuccessful endeavor. Although such effort indicates a motivated individual, the mentor may now be confronting someone who is so determined to charge straight ahead that selecting another option is somehow perceived as an admission of weakness. Any change in direction is viewed, not as the exercise of common sense and good judgment, but rather as failure.

In instances where the mentee's actions are inconsistent with achieving stated goals (which can occur for a variety of reasons), the

mentor should take a reasonably comprehensive approach to reviewing the status of the mentee's situation. In approaching the
mentee's problems from a broad perspective, the mentor would initiate the following four actions:

1. Provide important psychological and emotional support.

2. Examine the mentee's specific plans.

3. Evaluate the reasonable probability of success based on relevant facts such as required educational credentials, work-related
   experience, and training.

4. Explore the available options based on knowledge of the particular mentee.

REASONS FOR CURRENT PURSUITS

As part of the facilitation process, the mentor may need to
conduct a general review of the mentee's reasons for current educational and career pursuits. Some discussion regarding mentee
choices may certainly have occurred earlier, but not necessarily
with a direct focus on highlighting the mentee's specific and current reasons for choosing, or continuing to choose, particular academic, training, or work-related paths to follow as an adult learner.
The present-centered orientation will involve questions aimed at reviewing the more immediate issues, ideas, beliefs, and interests that
may have influenced the mentee and thus contributed significantly to
"here and now" intellectual and emotional responses.

A mentee could be impressed with an individual such as a
professor, executive, engineer, health professional, or social/political
activist who is a legitimate role model from a distance but with
whom the mentee has had either no direct or very limited personal
contact. The dedication and genuine interest an often highly visible person demonstrates toward a specific vocation may be quite
appealing to a relatively inexperienced mentee who may not fully
understand or be prepared to deal with the less attractive aspects
of some careers, such as the years of educational preparation and
training, the extended hours of work, the need for sophisticated

interpersonal, social, and political skills, or the ability to function within highly stressful environments.

The mentor can certainly assist the mentee by identifying opportunities, if possible, to obtain at least some (or more) relevant experience, so that the mentee might better develop a personal and realistic assessment of being a person in that position.

RECREATIONAL AND VOCATIONAL INTERESTS

In addition to the expected concerns regarding educational and career development, the mentor also could explore purely recreational as well as vocational interests which a mentee might view as important but clearly lesser priorities in terms of current commitments, energy, and time. Some mentees may already have developed personal pursuits which are either very focused or divided among a number of separate activities. As a result of the mentoring dialogue, the mentee may now recognize a significant opportunity for transforming a genuine interest in a specific recreational topic into a potential career or of creating a secondary or even primary source of income. For example, the whole range of hobbyist interests in handmade crafts—from holiday floral displays, to invitations based on calligraphy, to customized computer software and instruction—could be viewed as containing cottage industry commercial potential.

Of course, recreational interests do not need to connect with issues of livelihood. The mentor, for instance, may suggest that noncredit courses offered by educational institutions be considered as part of the mentee's exploration of intellectual, artistic, or physical sports-type endeavors. Many continuing education departments sponsor a diverse selection, covering subjects from astronomy, to dance, to comparative religion, to ceramics. In the workplace, the mentor could encourage the mentee to join skills-based associations devoted to improvement in public speaking and debate, as well as clubs focused on community service. A mentee could thus be motivated to continue an active and lifelong participation in a variety of individual interests and greatly benefit from such experiences with respect to personal enrichment, enjoyment, and social development.

However, there may be mentees who have few or no expressed interests outside of a single-minded dedication to educational or career pursuits. Certainly, for some mentees, given the status of their available resources, the decision to devote time and energy to achieving specific goals may be a wise decision. But the mentor can also introduce the view of continuing adult development as an opportunity to achieve a more balanced state of adulthood, with education, career, and recreational/social interests all as important components, if not necessarily equally relevant at the same time.

SUMMARY

To realistically enter into a substantive facilitative examination of options with a mentee, the mentor will need to rely on the knowledge and understanding gained from a reasonably well-established mentoring relationship. A mentor who was only involved in rather superficial interaction with a mentee would be hard pressed to explain the point of the facilitation. This explains why the term *facilitative* in the context of mentoring should be generally used to describe the mentor's behavioral interaction with the mentee *after* the relational and informational foundation has been created. Otherwise, what exactly would the mentor be facilitating? In pursuing a meaningful facilitative function, a mentor will employ a variety of approaches, and Figure 5.1 summarizes the means by which the mentee's journey can be extended into an enriched world of possibilities and alternatives.

Facilitative Focus

Guides mentees through a reasonably in-depth review and exploration of their interests, abilities, ideas, and beliefs

Purpose

To assist mentees in considering alternative views and options while
reaching their own decisions about attainable personal, academic,
and career objectives

Mentor Behaviors

* Pose hypothetical questions to expand individual views.
* Uncover the underlying experiential and informational basis for as-
  sumptions.
* Present multiple viewpoints to generate more in-depth analysis of
  decisions and options.
* Examine the seriousness of commitment to goals.
* Analyze reasons for current pursuits.
* Review recreational and vocational preferences.

Figure 5.1 Summary of facilitative focus function of mentor role.

CHAPTER 6

Engaging in Constructive Confrontation

In the constructive confrontation focus of mentoring, the mentor respectfully challenges students' or employees' explanations for or avoidance of decisions and actions relevant to their educational and career choices. The mentor attempts to assist mentees—as adult learners—to attain insight into unproductive strategies and behaviors and to reflect on their motivation and capacity to change. Because this approach contains potential benefits as well as risks to the mentee and the ongoing relationship, a vital concern for the mentor will be the determination of both the issues and the timing of remarks appropriate for a confrontive intervention (Hammond, Hepworth, & Smith, 1977).

In general, the confrontive function places the mentor in the position of stating that the mentee's commitments to, or specific strategies and actions for, resolving an education or career related concern are not consistent with the mentee's *own* expressed view of the problem *as a priority*. However, without some degree of meaningful trust as the interpersonal baseline, a mentee may not either accept or profit from the mentor's confrontive comments, especially if the mentee is initially rather sensitive about the problem. It will not matter how well-intentioned and on-target the advice is relevant to the mentee's personal situation. In fact, an important overall concern should be that any of the behaviors of confrontation, especially if introduced too early and forcefully into the mentoring dialogue, could jeopardize the probability of a successful relationship from continuing beyond that point.

An important assumption, therefore, in the mentoring model is that a confrontive approach is probably ineffective and even counterproductive as a practical means of creating collaborative learning until a reasonably well-established and continuing relational, informational, and facilitative relationship has been developed between the mentor and the mentee. Although some mentees may maturely handle and immediately benefit from a mentor's challenge to reflect on their current problem-solving strategies without a substantive base of prior relational and informational mentoring interaction, the mentor should carefully consider the psychological *receptivity* of each mentee before embarking on a confrontive encounter. Often, a more gradual rather than a too rapid and overly intimidating advance would be a prudent initial approach. The goal is to maximize the positive and minimize the negative consequences of interaction within the boundaries of confrontation.

Taking adequate time to establish a climate of psychological and emotional support and to obtain relevant factual knowledge about the particular mentee is a prerequisite for the creation of trust. If a mentee initially interprets the mentor's intentions as that of a superior adult attempting to tell a subordinate adult—who may be a relative stranger—what to think, how to feel, and what to do, then a mentee could easily react to any advice offered in this context by feeling pressured and controlled. The mentee would thus be repelled from rather than attracted to the mentoring relationship. Such a resentful response would obviously reduce the ability of the mentee to engage in meaningful interpersonal interaction and diminish the intrinsic value of the mentor's original observations and perceptions as an important source of assistance for the mentee.

As the relationship develops, it is therefore critical that the mentor reinforces the mutual understanding that advice is not a command, and that mentees must personally decide whether to accept confrontive recommendations. Mentees may sometimes feel pressured to say "yes" or believe they are viewed as resistant if they say "no." The mentor may inadvertently overdo the attempt to offer valuable guidance, but the mentor can counteract this problem by openly encouraging the mentee to politely remind the mentor that the final responsibility for utilizing advice, as they have agreed, is the mentee's.

By occasionally reemphasizing what might appear to be a simple point—that the mentee will ultimately benefit or not from simple point—that the mentee will ultimately benefit or not from the consequences of all decisions—the mentor can reinforce the mentee's right to be assertive about deciding when and if to act on advice from anyone, including the mentor. In offering this sometimes necessary corrective emphasis, especially to mentees who might be less likely to speak up unless directly asked, the mentor can help to ensure that confrontive mentor behaviors do not improperly influence a mentee. The mentor certainly does not want a mentee to drift (or feel pushed) in the direction of unrealistically expecting the mentor to be the one who can or should actually make choices that *only* the mentee can make as an independent adult learner.

In considering the factors of mentee receptivity and the timing of remarks, the mentor could conclude that delaying a confrontive intervention would be the best option. However, there is the risk that at some point, by not confronting clearly unproductive mentee behaviors and strategies, the opposite unintended message could be sent—that all mentee decisions and actions are acceptable, workable, and will realistically provide the desired outcomes.

The mentor, therefore, may sometimes be in the position of deciding between less than crystal clear intervention alternatives. In considering the possibilities, the mentor must recognize the implications of mentor action or inaction: there will be consequences for saying and doing something, and there will be consequences for saying and doing nothing—but either way there will be consequences to the mentee. For the mentor, the issue of intervention may essentially be reduced to a focused question: Do the benefits of successfully engaging in confrontive behaviors with the mentee outweigh the possible risks to the mentee and to the mentoring relationship itself?

In attempting to use confrontation as a constructive part of the process of significant mentoring interaction, a mentor should consider the following six approaches:

1. Use careful probing to assess psychological readiness of the mentee to benefit from different points of view.

2. Make an open acknowledgment of concerns about possible negative consequences of constructive feedback on the relationship.

3. Employ a confrontive verbal stance aimed at the primary goal of promoting self-assessment of apparent discrepancies.

4. Focus on most likely strategies and behaviors for meaningful change.

5. Use the least amount of carefully stated feedback necessary for impact.

6. Offer comments (before and after confrontive remarks) to reinforce belief in positive potential for mentee growth beyond the current situation.

READINESS TO CONSIDER DIFFERENT VIEWS

The mentor may need to probe carefully in determining the strength of the mentee's present intellectual and emotional attachments to ideas and beliefs and not just assume a genuine readiness to seriously consider other options. Views anchored firmly in past experiences and reinforced by family and peer groups may appear to some mentees as not particularly debatable, and the attempt by the mentor to ask questions could be interpreted as an intrusion into quite personal and sacred turf.

The open mind approach literally requires a genuine receptivity to the learning potential offered by exploring differences. A mentee will often need to experience, by active participation with a mentor, this type of challenging interaction to really appreciate the process of objective examination of diverse points of view. Mentees who may not fully recognize the value of considering the world of options, nor even initially accept the premise that other legitimate cognitive approaches and affective responses are always possible, can thus be exposed to this expanded reality through the healthy opportunity of challenge in a supportive context.

The mentor in education, for example, might recommend a course in multicultural and gender-related topics to a mentee who really could benefit, personally as well as professionally, from considering other views. A mentee in the workplace might be asked to consider some voluntary training or workshops in cultural diversity sponsored by the organization, which the mentee had previously assumed to be unnecessary or unimportant. The point would be to challenge a mentee to experience, as an adventure in learning, other unexamined cognitive and affective dimensions of facts, perception, and reactions.

In these instances, however, some mentees may not suddenly ignite with enthusiasm at the prospect of responding to such direct recommendations. The mentor can certainly suggest that the issue be reexamined after the mentee has considered or even researched the specific value of the subject. Moreover, this facet of mentoring should not imply that the mentor must openly confront *all* views or opinions the mentee expresses during the mentoring interaction.

Instead, the mentor should carefully select significant issues related to the mentee's educational and career growth. If the situation warrants, the mentor may sometimes need to risk challenging a mentee's reasoning and facts even if the mentee appears unreceptive, because the mentor's overall role is to meaningfully assist the development of mentees rather than to merely please them by avoiding difficult but relevant topics.

For example, a mentee whose academic record reveals poor overall performance fairly early in the semester, might still insist on maintaining a full load of courses instead of reviewing other options, such as withdrawing immediately from one and concentrating on the remaining subjects. This mentee may need to be directly confronted by the mentor in order to specifically pin down the advantages and disadvantages of such an approach. In some instances, the mentee may have seen the problem as resolvable in that a course or two could be dropped at the deadline later in the semester, but not have considered the possible error in judgment of continuing to split time and energy resources too thin. The mentor might point out that this plan could, by the deadline, reduce the opportunity for success in the remaining courses. Of course, there clearly would be other options as well, and the mentor's goal would be to help the mentee arrive at the most effective solution by directly confronting the issue, instead of simply allowing the mentee to retreat into less workable or desirable actions.

The mentor will need to demonstrate real interpersonal skill and judgment to ensure that the mentee benefits from the confrontive interaction as intended. Testing for readiness, which always needs to be respectful, sometimes needs as well to be a recurrent behavioral activity. And knowing when to back off, when to remain in the same place, and when to move or push forward is an essential component of the *art* of mentoring.

IMPACT OF MENTOR FEEDBACK ON RELATIONSHIP

As the mentoring relationship evolves, the mentor will want to be perceived as a person in the positive advocacy role of looking out for the best interests of the mentee. When introducing confrontive remarks into the dialogue, the mentor can often lessen the potential negative impact of what is clearly intended as constructive feedback by openly expressing concern to the mentee about the effects of such remarks on the relationship. By sometimes verbalizing a concern for the mentee's anticipated response, the mentor can alleviate the tension of confrontive interaction.

This approach should encourage the mentee to view the mentor as as advocate and thus prepare the mentee to react more objectively to constructive critiques about educational and career development. In essence, the mentor's specific feedback is aimed not only at the creative intellectual exploration of the mentee's talents, but also at openly communicating confidence in the ability of the mentee to develop and succeed in realistic pursuits. The importance of expressing *positive expectations* to the mentee should not be underestimated.

Of course, if a particular mentee demonstrates an especially mature ability to use the advice of confrontation, then the mentor can be alert to, but less overtly concerned about, the need to explain the goodwill behind the remarks. In fact, some mentees could even resent the suggestion that they require legitimate mentor critique to be delivered in a package of continual reassurance.

Certainly, mentees should not be viewed as candidates for endless emotional spoon-feeding of the overly solicitous variety, which could clearly suggest a patronizing attitude by the mentor.

However, there will be occasions when the mentor's patience and expressed genuine concern about remaining a positive influence could help those mentees who, because of inexperience with the learning value of confrontive dialogue, react too quickly to feedback as a type of personal criticism. If the mentor can assist the mentee to fixate less on ego defense and more on personal growth potential, then the mentoring relationship can be a vital source of reflection which enhances the mentee's ability to pursue lifelong learning.

The mentor will need to decide, as the mentoring relationship evolves, on the most effective strategy for each mentee, given the issues involved, the point in the relationship, and the specific personality of each mentee.

SELF-ASSESSMENT OF DISCREPANCIES

A central purpose of confrontation is to point out discrepancies and inconsistencies between the mentee's stated goals and those significant actions required to accomplish them. After the mentee has established a plan for reaching certain objectives, the mentor can assist as an alter ego to reflect—through the eyes of an experienced traveller—the status of the mentee's progress during that phase of the developmental journey. In this role, however, the mentor must be careful to be more a concerned monitor of progress and less a judge.

Certainly, a mentor's perception will prove valuable to the extent that it provides an accurate factual assessment of the mentee's various steps on the path toward defined goals. But the mentor must also be concerned with motivating the mentee to continue the journey. Mentors, therefore, cannot effectively function merely as neutral or detached observers. They must consciously remember to acknowledge, support, and praise positive effort and not dwell only on achievement. In addition, changing and even uncertain mentee interests should be welcomed and accepted as healthy exploration, not immediately interpreted as the confusion of the immature or inexperienced.

Such obvious problems as documented lack of significant

progress should be a necessary topic of constructive mentoring dialogue. Mentees can then be assisted to pragmatically consider ways in which they might either improve the probabilities of success on their originally chosen pathways or reconsider alternatives. As an illustration of this approach, a mentor could state that a mentee who has worked diligently and attended classes, and even sought additional tutoring, but received less than the hoped-for grades, *has* demonstrated the commitment required for achievement. But after a careful review, the mentor might also then suggest that the particular content of the field selected for study does not appear to be really suitable to the mentee's aptitudes and/or prior academic preparation (such as math or science).

The mentor could then help the mentee decide about the possibility of redirecting such a praiseworthy commitment of time and energy to a more attainable goal. The mentee could also be referred for counseling so that a professional more acquainted with the specifics of aptitude assessment and career decision making could provide an expert and comprehensive opinion. The success of such confrontive mentor behaviors, as well as the assistance offered by other professionals, will depend on the readiness and ability of mentees to accept a realworld evaluation of their educational and career progress.

To some mentees, mentors may appear to be offering less than flattering assessments of the mentees' reasons for explaining a downward learning or performance curve. At such points, the prior relational, informational, and facilitative foundation will need to be relied upon to help counterbalance the weight of the confrontive points. The strength of the already established mentoring relationship should now provide the general mutual respect and trust that will enable the sometimes rough edges of confrontive interaction to be less intrusive as an interpersonal barrier.

In reviewing and referencing a mentee's record to clarify specific details, a mentor may need to provide direct feedback aimed at carefully penetrating the mentee's generalized and sometimes vague explanations for problems. A mentee, for example, could explain a performance problem as a lack of ability to judge "how much work" many academic courses or workplace projects demand, or as a difficulty "to find the time." Such explanations are often, in fact, initially offered as the reasons for the inability to complete essential educational or workplace tasks as varied as thorough textbook review, research papers, laboratory experiments, or job assignments involving critical dates.

The mentor could certainly acknowledge (if this is the case) that the mentee appears to have the aptitude and talent to perform well or even excel in an academic or career field. Then the focus should shift to the empirical evidence—the mentee is still receiving less than the required grades or performance evaluations— especially if a higher overall profile of accomplishment will be required to successfully achieve the mentee's goals. In such instances, a mentor could help by first openly recognizing the mentee's personal disappointment in being in an obviously difficult and frustrating position. The mentor could then assist the mentee to examine the anticipated consequences of continuing along the same path by specifically inquiring as to the mentee's view of the seriousness of the situation, and what options (if any) are being considered by the mentee to correct the problem.

The more the mentor can center the dialogue on reality-based alternatives and reasonable solutions, the more the mentee will experience the mentoring relationship as a personally positive growth opportunity and less as an unintended and negative judgment and prediction about limitations. After sufficient discussions about a mentee's lack of achievement, if the mentor is unable to offer any workable suggestions, then the mentor should consider referring the mentee to another organizational resource or professional with special expertise who is more suited to access the persistent discrepancy between the mentee's stated goals, abilities, and performance.

Mentees need direct feedback about how they are doing *now* on their chosen journey, as well as estimates about how far they might finally travel.

CHANGING STRATEGIES AND BEHAVIORS

A mentee's difficulties and problems relevant to progress in fulfilling education, training, and career plans could be accounted for by multiple causes, and a mentor can help the mentee identify those issues and problems appropriate for continued discussion within the mentoring relationship. As Schlossberg, Lynch, and Chickering (1989) relate:

> It is easy to identify things that upset you; what's hard is deciding what to do about your feelings and the situations that give rise to them. Confronting very challenging transitions often makes people feel helpless and therefore hopeless. They may feel that they have little control over their *Situation* and that their options are few. But in fact there are almost always more *Strategies* than people realize. Sociologist Leonard Pearlin tells us that there is no single, magic-bullet coping strategy. The effective coper is someone who can use many *Strategies* flexibly, depending on the *Situation*. (p. 65)

Sometimes, a mentor's initial contribution can be helping the mentee to acknowledge and start dealing with the reasons for a problem—the vital first steps. But mentors will not only explore potential based on the mentee's interests, needs, and capabilities, they will also face the *limits of change* within the boundaries of mentoring. The mentor, therefore, will often need to assist the mentee as well in selecting those strategies and behaviors which appear most capable of productive change by the mentee.

Mentors will certainly want to remain tuned to those "teachable moments" (Havighurst, 1972) in which mentees openly indicate that there is a self-identified opportunity for their motivation and learning to naturally merge. A mentee, for example, who asserts, "This is a great time for me to learn this," is certainly offering clear signals about the possibility of making a serious commitment to pursue a goal. However, a mentor should also suggest, as additional opportunities for learning, those subjects or competencies worthy of consideration about which the mentee has not directly expressed any interest.

A mentee in education, for instance, who is enthusiastic about quantitative areas such as statistics or economics, but reveals little concern for personal or professional development in the humanities or psychological sciences, could be asked about the influence of these distinct preferences in limiting or expanding present and future opportunities. And the mentee who has avoided science, business, or technology-based subjects in favor of the arts and humanities should be asked as well to consider the impact of this exclusive mindset on the potential for personal development as a balanced individual, worker, and citizen.

Within the workplace, the mentor can utilize the same confrontive focus approach to deal with the gap, for example, between a mentee's verbal and behavioral support. A mentee who is publicly behind introducing team process models of functioning into an organization as a means of increasing productivity, yet shows little actual personal commitment to helping the staff promote any of their internal efforts at integrating such team models, may need such a discrepancy pointed out. As an important idea for discussion, the mentor may inquire about the mentee's view regarding the active responsibility of employees at every level to maintain, nurture, and enhance the overall organization's competency to compete in the marketplace. The mentor can also indicate that others have noted the mentee's reluctance to participate, and then raise the probable effect of such a negative perception on mentee advancement.

Of course, the mentor's role is to encourage the mentee to examine the functional value of topics of direct interest, as well as to broaden the current perspective of the mentee by including a more expanded view of adult learning. As an illustration, a mentor could challenge a mentee who holds the rather narrow mindset of education as simply a marketable commodity to instead consider the value of lifelong learning as a continuing activity encompassing many different but equally important opportunities for both individual and career development.

The challenge is to see learning and training as more of a personally evolving and adaptive process based on anticipated change, and less as a belief in a fixed map drawn by someone else of permanent educational and career signs that clearly mark the trail mentees are to follow. This approach can lead to an expansion of the mentee's own capability to pursue reasonable and important self-initiated changes in strategies or behaviors. The following observation by Naisbitt and Adburdene (1990) is relevant to those employees or managers who need to reexamine their workplace assumptions:

The primary challenge of leadership in the 1990's is to encourage the new, better-educated worker to be more entrepreneurial, self-managing, and oriented toward lifelong learning. (p. 242)

Of course, the mentor should not unilaterally approach the change process as something to be imposed on the mentee. Instead, the mentor will rely on the accumulated knowledge about the particular mentee as the primary source of determining which issues are realistically amenable to change. The range of problems to be considered could in fact mirror many of the important issues raised within the continuing relationship, information, and facilitative dimensions of mentoring, but now be more properly and directly addressed from the confrontive perspective.

USE OF MINIMUM FEEDBACK

The purpose of the mentor's feedback is to elicit genuine cooperation and to stimulate sincere interest by the mentee in pursuing opportunities for meaningful educational, training, and career development. After the mutual identification, for example, of a problem the mentee has decided to devote time and energy to solving, the mentor must address another significant concern—the actual quantity of critique-based information that is reasonable and helpful to include in the mentoring dialogue.

Generally, the mentor should use the least amount of critical feedback necessary for impact in the attempt to assist the mentee through the process of self-development. The mentor will need to be direct and factual in order to provide the examples necessary for the mentee to fully understand the mentor's concerns. But the mentor should also avoid engaging the mentee in too much analysis of the microspecifics of personal assessment. By offering example after example of the same problem, an excess of data can overwhelm the main point and create a condition of inadvertent informational or psychological overload. The mentor will also need to avoid raising too many separate issues in the relatively short span of a single mentoring session for the mentee to practically consider at one time.

The mentor should certainly offer an ongoing assessment of competencies clearly necessary for continued mentee development. However, the mentor should base such proposed improvement action plans on a real-world review of both successful and unsuccessful past mentee efforts in educational, training, or career endeavors. The overall purpose is to tailor assessment-type comments and guidelines to each mentee's particular situation so that the mentee both recognizes the important progress which has occurred, as well as understands the necessary actions upon which additional learning will depend for continued improvement in the targeted areas.

Moreover, the mentor should generally offer comments that acknowledge and praise the mentee's genuine efforts as an open recognition of the hard work involved, regardless of the degree to which the time and energy expended have produced positive results. In these instances, the mentor's positive and sensitive approach to enhancing the mentee's self-esteem and motivation will often be crucial in promoting genuine mentee receptivity to feedback. Assessment is neither meant to be sugarcoated optimism nor unfounded pessimism, but instead supportive and factual advice offered for mature consideration by the mentee—to be accepted, modified, or rejected.

Usually, the mentor can help to more effectively evaluate progress toward the educational and career goals established by the mentee by determining the criteria being used as the measure of success. In fact, the mentor will often need to precisely clarify what progress means from the perspective of the mentee, especially when referring to areas of learning that appear to reveal less than anticipated results. Mentees may have definite subjective views for measuring achievement which may or may not be based on realistic qualitative, quantitative, or time frame expectations. Sometimes, the mentee may therefore believe that the mentor is being overly polite or not polite enough, and the mentor's specific comments about the mentee's extent of progress may introduce some heightened tension, and even lead to healthy disagreements regarding mentor-mentee perceptions.

The mentor may need to assist the mentee in surfacing a variety of powerful (but often verbally unexpressed) myths which can undermine the potential for learning. Two such beliefs are that early lack of success automatically disqualifies a person from further achievement or that reliance on willpower alone—which confuses self-pride with the unproductive refusal to seek assistance—will somehow still produce the miracle of as yet unattained goals. Often, an important part of mentee development will involve learning how to maintain stability by pragmatically interpreting progress. The mentor should review with a mentee why extreme and prolonged negative overreactions can seriously diminish rather than enhance the discovery potential of the developmental journey, especially in situations involving varying degrees of success.

BELIEF IN MENTEE POTENTIAL

Critiques can have an unsettling effect on a mentee. The mentor can assist the mentee in maintaining the equilibrium necessary for pursuing the *self-correction* component of trial and error learning by offering positive comments, before and after the feedback, to reinforce belief in the mentee's potential for growth beyond the present situation.

Without offering false reassurance, an essential mentor message should be that personal determination to continue striving for positive outcomes, even when success is uncertain or distant, is often a major variable in achieving *the possible*. Although motivation may not be a guarantee, it usually is an essential ingredient in achievement. By coupling sound advice with a positive belief in the mentee's potential for improvement, the mentor's encouraging view will itself often serve as an important influence.

In addition, the mentor should be alert to offering comments which encourage the pursuit of attainable and valued competencies at a pace consistent with the unique learning style of each mentee. For some mentees, the mentor may need to emphasize that there is not some ideal model of mentee behavior or progress to which they are, or should be, compared. The mentor should inquire as to the mentees' own perception of themselves as adult learners. The internalized model against which mentees are judging their own progress may be based on an unrealistic view of the serious mentee as an almost perfect adult learner—who can be completely responsible for immediate, substantive, and simultaneous improvements.

Often, the mentor's objective will be to challenge the mentee to identify sensible standards for evaluating progress, which can then be used as proper baseline indicators for discussing concerns relevant to academic and career development. Some mentees who refer to themselves as having high standards may require assistance in distinguishing "high" from "unreal." Other mentees are truly spread thin among educational, career, and family responsibilities, but still insist on unfairly and harshly criticizing themselves for less than sterling achievement.

Hypercritical personal evaluation will sometimes depend more on mentee self-feedback (the "internal judge") as the source of discontent, and less on the mentee's expectations of self as imposed by the requirements of others, though there clearly may be a direct and interactive correlation. The mentee's capability to engage in constructive self-assessment as well as the ability to maturely respond to the legitimate critiques provided by others may therefore need review. Proficiency in both types of learning can be a significant influence on adult development.

Generally, the mentor should offer the mentee a balanced critique to ensure that compliments about significant improvements, as well as concerns about problems in performance, are viewed as equally important *facts*. Mentees can undervalue their achievement as well as overvalue it, and a mentor should anticipate the need to carefully address such distortions in mentee perception. An approach which includes the assessment of both strengths and weaknesses will usually provide more comprehensive feedback to the mentee, and thereby serve as a more valuable source for the realistic evaluation of learning. In addition, mentees with real self-doubts about their own abilities will usually benefit from the mentor's continuing reinforcement of belief in the them as capable adult learners. Often, such faith will prove to be the charge necessary to energize and sustain their constructive actions as they explore the world of their own potential.

SUMMARY

The underlying rationale for the general use of mentor-initiated confrontation is that the mentor perceives a clear *discrepancy* between the mentee's stated objectives and the mentee's demonstrated commitment or progress toward the attainment of personal, educational, training, and career goals. This type of mentor-mentee interpersonal interaction is not similar to the more conventional argumentative style associated with the typical personality clash. Instead, the helping behaviors of the confrontive function are consistent with the intent of mentors who are openly but patiently trying to address unresolved mentee problems and to identify workable solutions. Of course, the mentor's attempt to focus on discrepancy factors may create some interpersonal friction, because the mentee may not always be receptive to or comfortable with the mentor's determined initiative to surface particular issues which the mentee thus far has kept at a conscious distance through avoidance or denial.

Because the confrontive style could disrupt the ongoing mentoring relationship, the mentor must be especially careful to have attended to the previous phases (relationship, informative, and facilitative) to minimize a possible negative mentee reaction. Although there is always some probability of an initial mentee overreaction, without a reasonable level of established trust, the mentor could risk the type of serious backlash which might damage the further value of the mentoring relationship. Figure 6.1 highlights the techniques which the mentor can use to effectively incorporate confrontive focus behaviors into the mentoring relationship.

Confrontive Focus

Respectfully challenges mentees' explanations for or avoidance of decisions and actions relevant to their development as adult learners

Purpose

To help mentees attain insight into unproductive behaviors and to evaluate their need and capacity to change

Mentor Behaviors

* Use careful probing to assess psychological readiness of the mentee to benefit from different points of view.
* Make an open acknowledgment of concerns about possible negative consequences of constructive ("critical") feedback on the relationship.
* Employ a confrontive verbal stance aimed at the primary goal of promoting self-assessment of apparent discrepancies.
* Focus on most likely strategies and behaviors for meaningful change.
* Use the least amount of carefully stated feedback necessary for impact.
* Offer comments (before and after confrontive remarks) to reinforce belief in positive potential for mentee growth beyond the current situation.

Figure 6.1 Summary of the confrontive focus function of mentor role.

CHAPTER 7

Sharing Yourself as a Role Model

In the traditional role model concept, the responsibility for learning primarily remains with the individual who is drawn to the status and qualities possessed by another person. Although there may be some limited contact or involvement, the role model does not need to consciously volunteer to engage in any activities or conversations with the "beneficiary," who may be influenced solely by observation. By contrast, in the mentoring model, mentors assume responsibility for being functional role models because they choose to develop mutual relationships that require personal commitments of their time and energy for the purpose of benefiting mentees.

Mentors also explicitly participate as active role models with mentees by sharing appropriate life experiences in order to personalize and enrich ongoing relationships. The mentors' selective self-disclosure of psychological and emotional reactions to events in their own lives—which is then related to the mentees' present situation—becomes an integral part of the mentoring relationship. This often enables mentees to approach the analysis of current problems and the exploration of feasible solutions with a more insightful, pragmatic, and confident perspective.

Generally, mentees enter into the mentoring relationship with the reasonable belief that mentors will offer important and competent guidance in helping them to reach some tangible objective, whether the goal is related to an education, training, or career agenda. Mentees rely on mentors to offer meaningful assistance in their own development because mentors represent knowledge, skills, and proficiencies the mentees also desire, but which are beyond their own present level of experience and attainment.

The parties would not refer to themselves as a mentor (primarily the educator) and a mentee (primarily the learner) if both parties were equally competent in the significant areas selected for mentoring. Certainly, peer mentoring interactions allow an important exchange of learning to occur between coequals. However, such relationships are not directly relevant to the psychology of adult mentoring because the primary, and usually transitional, active role model is *neither parent nor peer*.

The mentor model function is particularly valuable to the mentee because it provides an opportunity for a special type of individualized learning between an adult *educator* and an adult *learner*, whether in academia, business, or government. As a participant role model, the mentor can attempt to maximize the potential to be a positive motivational influence by using the following five approaches as a means of effectively integrating the mentor model component into the mentoring relationship:

1. Offer personal thoughts and genuine feelings to emphasize the value of learning from unsuccessful or difficult experiences (as trial-and-error, and self-correction, and not as growth-limiting "failures").

2. Select related examples from own life (and experiences as mentor of other mentees) based on probable motivational value.

3. Provide a direct, realistic assessment of positive belief in mentee's ability to pursue attainable goals.

4. Express a confident view of appropriate risk taking as necessary for personal, educational, training, and career development.

5. Make statements that clearly encourage personal mentee actions to attain stated objectives.

LEARNING FROM DIFFICULT EXPERIENCES

During their own journey, mentees usually need reassurance in maintaining commitment, discipline, and motivation in the continuing effort to manage and override anxiety and fear of failure. The mentor's own self-disclosure regarding personal strategies for handling difficult experiences can provide an inspirational example for most mentees. Mentees will benefit by being reminded that "doubt" and "deficiency" are not synonymous, and that quite successful persons—like mentors—also have had to contend with discouragement and to overcome obstacles on the path toward their goals.

Mentees will vary in their capacity to appreciate the survival and achievement stories offered as insight. In fact, their specific ability to benefit from the mentor model of learning-from-shared-experiences may be quite different. However, the majority of mentees will be reasonably receptive to the mentor's *underlying* point—that our society, in using the word *success* as the traditional benchmark to describe a positive outcome of learning, has also unfortunately used the cutoff word *failure* to demean and inaccurately define all praiseworthy effort which did not result in an especially recordable success.

To repair the often considerable damage caused by this corrosive idea, mentors should vigorously communicate to mentees a more affirmative, accurate, and essential explanation:

- Only continued exploration of potential will allow mentees to discover what their competencies really are.
- Lack of specific accomplishment in a particular area—though often a painful fact—should not be interpreted and internalized as generalized failure, but rather as constructive feedback from the exciting though often stressful world of developmental possibility.

This approach is not meant to minimize or rationalize away the difficult to absorb personal impact created by lack of success, but rather to utilize a wide range of experiences as a source of meaningful adult learning. The mentor can thereby establish a dialogue with the mentee in which the *value* of both "success" and "failure" to promote active learning is realistically examined.

In the mutual attempt to locate the wisdom contained in what clearly appear to be unsuccessful endeavors, the mentor should generally anticipate cooperation instead of unreasonable resistance. Most mentees will view the adult education–adult learner relationship as a productive opportunity to learn rather than as a major learner dependency problem. Mentees expect mentors to help them extract important wisdom from their experiences, and they view mentors as possessing the necessary combination of maturity and skill to find meaning in complexity.

Mentors, therefore, in the early mentoring interaction should be especially careful about overreacting to mentees' allusions to the implied competency difference between them, often conveyed by terms which describe the mentor as more "intelligent," "wise," or "insightful." Those mentors who are uncomfortable in the role of the more knowledgeable and experienced superior within a one-to-one relationship should be particularly alert to the risk of incorrectly translating a mentee's initial attitude of "I am an adult learner here to learn from you—the adult educator" into the quite different message of "I am an adult learner—a truly dependent person of inferior status—here to learn from a superior person."

Mentors should not initiate and then pursue a dialogue with mentees based on the assumption that the proficiency inequality aspect of mentoring will inescapably trigger burning issues about authority or self-esteem. Adult learner attitudes about being in the position of "the helped," if expressed, do not necessarily indicate unhealthy mentee dependency. The mentee may only be referring to the obvious status distinction between a professor and student, or senior manager and junior employee.

Also, by overly focusing them on the need for the mentor-mentee relationship to operate as an interaction between equals, mentors could divert mentees away from the merit of reflecting on lessons learned from past experiences. Mentees could become confused instead of enlightened about the legitimate role of the mentor as the educator in the mentoring experience, and even interpret the overemphasis on learner equality as a puzzling and even patronizing false sincerity.

Usually, adult mentees do not respond to one-to-one learning by being literally reduced to the status of *subordinates*, and as a result, suffering the detrimental impact of lowered personal self-esteem and weakened motivation. In reality, as Brookfield (1991) observed regarding the need by adult learners to respect the credibility of the individual in the teacher role:

> Learners repeatedly stress the wish to be in the presence of someone who is perceived as having greater factual knowledge, skill mastery, and reasoning facility than they (the learners) possess. . . . Teachers may believe that in saying "look, my own experience possesses no greater innate validity than yours" that they are encouraging in learners a valuing of their own experiences. In actuality, exactly the reverse can happen. . . . Hence, it is important that in our desire to affirm the validity of learners' own experiences and abilities, we do not undercut our own credibility in their eyes. (p. 52)

However, if the mentor believes the mentoring relationship is reinforcing a dependency which could seriously interefere with the mentee's development as a self-directed, independent adult learner, the mentor could request additional expertise regarding the most effective strategies for intervention with the mentee. Although mentors must address the self-worth problems raised by mentees who truly view themselves as *inferior people*, the mentors' responses should not result in actions that devalue their own continuing mentoring effectiveness. The mentor and a counselor or other mental health professional, for instance, could work together to assist the mentee in different but equally valuable ways.

Also, if the mentor-mentee relationship dynamic of educator-as-superior and learner-as-subordinate creates a serious interpersonal authority barrier for a particular mentee, which is openly expressed through negative behaviors, the mentor may need to refer the individual to a professional specifically trained to provide more specialized assistance. Serious personal issues can occur for many reasons beyond the scope of the mentor's ability to handle or resolve alone—from unresolved conflict with authority figures to the baggage of a poor self-concept. Regardless of the mentor's speculation as to the actual cause of the mentee's inappropriate or ineffective behavior, a referral should definitely be considered if the mentor faces continuous mentee anger or anticipates the possibility of further contributing to the mentee's condition of situational dependency.

The mentor's self-disclosure contains power because of its ability to reinforce a credible *competency-oriented* model of continual learning—of goals pursued despite individual uncertainties, obstacles, and setbacks. The mentor should express concern if there is any evidence of unthinking and self-limiting mentee actions. Two indicators are withdrawal responses from difficult situations or a factual history that the mentee, encouraged by others, pursued but did not achieve personal success in educational and career opportunities which were presented as viable opportunities. Such a background could now block mentee receptivity to suggestions. The alert mentor will review the mentee's current decisions about pursuing or avoiding new learning possibilities, because the mentee may be looking more for a guarantee of success than for anything else.

Mentors can assist mentees by encouraging them to take reasonable risks (certainly from the mentees' point of view) and to continue overcoming difficulties in their educational and career paths.

MOTIVATIONAL VALUE OF EXAMPLES

A practical guideline for selecting mentor history to share should be the motivational value offered by connecting actual examples to present mentee concerns. As an illustration, the mentor's stories about personal struggles to overcome obstacles are used to create a foundation of experience which is drawn from the hard lessons of difficult and even unsuccessful events. But for the shared examples to be of real worth, the mentor must first screen them through the filter of anticipated motivational impact on the mentee, especially since the mentor's primary intention is to help sustain the mentee through similar problems.

For the recognized superior in the relationship, self-disclosure immediately raises another important issue. In sharing personal thoughts and emotions (doubt as well as confidence) relevant to achievement in the face of difficulty, the mentor may have some concern about diminishing what could be perceived as the useful luster of being an idealized role model. Could the mentee now be too easily dismissive of the guidance of a mentor who proves to be less than perfect?

In actuality, the tough behind-the-scenes reality of the mentor's own history is exactly what should be shared with mentees. The mentor's own struggle to realize dreams is not allowed to remain as some imagined tale which occurred in the abstract realm of incredible luck or fantasized easy achievement; the mentor certainly does not wish to be viewed as an idealized person for whom success was almost magically guaranteed. Rather, the actual story has genuine relevance because the mentor now shares selected ideas and emotions that apply to the mentee's own world of personal, educational, and career development.

In determining which autobiographical events have motivational relevance, the mentor should base the choices less on the comparability of actual details and more on the *meaning* as interpreted by the mentor for the mentee. It is unlikely that the mentor's specific experiences will (or need to) exactly parallel the mentee's; the real importance is the transfer of learning to the mentee that the shared experience represents, not the details. The emphasis of the lesson is on *attitude*. The point is not that a mentee must imitate or duplicate the mentor's situation-specific solutions, but instead that the mentee can also discover reasonably workable, if not perfect, solutions to most problems.

In addition, the mentor may need to demystify a variety of mentee beliefs. Some mentees may reference the allegedly streamlined and relatively stress-free educational and career achievements of other persons, whom they believe, unlike themselves, live within a charmed circle and have success bestowed upon them. The mentor may need to emphasize the real issue, which is the willingness of the mentee to make the same pragmatic commitment required by the great majority (granted some silver-spoon exceptions) of other people who are serious about undertaking and sustaining the hard work required for optimal performance.

Such a dialogue may also need to include a serious review of the personal expectations of many inexperienced adult learners. Due to their unrealistic assumptions about ideal conditions for learning, they often react to the usual problems within the imperfect worlds of both education and the workplace as an "unfairness" specifically directed against them. If the mentor can help the mentee to minimize any counterproductive emotional overinvestment in the distractions created by these normal difficulties, then the mentor's shared experiences may truly provide meaningful ballast for the mentee. Of course, if problems exist which are patently unfair and unreasonable, the mentor and mentee can mutually pursue the proper actions and seek a just resolution.

In helping to plan and examine those details appropriate for each mentee's unique approach to handling current issues, the mentor needs to maintain a reasonable objectivity. A mentor must be able to recognize, especially during the intensity of the mentoring interaction, that the mentor's own personal preferences about how to engage in problem-solving actions may not always correspond to the mentee's own behavioral style of coping.

It is vital that the mentoring dialogue remains clearly *centered* on the details of the mentee's personal, educational, and career real-world situation because these are the specifics that *now* matter. As Wlodkowski (1990) noted:

> Most psychologists use the word *motivation* to describe those processes that can energize behavior and give direction or purpose to behavior. When we consider the human functions in learning, such as attention, concentration, effort, perseverance, and initiative, we are dealing with motivational processes that are activated and sustained through human energy. *What* we pay attention to or expend our energy upon deals with the directional aspect of human motivation. Since human energy is finite . . . we constantly have to shift our attention and effort to cope with the world around us. Thus, there is a dynamic interaction between what is going on within us, such as needs, feelings, and memories, with what is going on outside of us, such as the many environmental attractions and influences in our daily lives. (pp. 97–98)

Certainly, mentors properly attempt to energize, focus, and guide mentees into positive action by selectively sharing their own past experiences and then carefully connecting them to the real needs of mentees. Sometimes, however, the goals of the mentor model may be difficult to attain, especially when mentees enter into mentoring relationships with self-limiting ideas about what to expect from the mentor. The mentee with a preconceived image of the person in the mentor role as primarily that of the comforting authority figure may be willing to be a silent partner. As a result, such a mentee could prefer to quickly retreat into the unchallenged acceptance of the mentor's views, or desire to continue recreating the passive, risk-avoidant, less personally visible activities of prior learning situations.

Mentors need to be alert to mentees who are overly invested in such narrow expectations, because if not corrected, these beliefs could clearly reduce the mentees' genuine opportunities to learn from mentoring interactions. The self-disclosure component can provide motivational assistance to the mentee. And the mentor can be a positive influence by modeling another type of learning that is often necessary for the personal development of many mentees—the understanding that one's own attainments as an adult are revealed by mature confidence, not inappropriate discomfort or offensive arrogance.

Usually, the mentee's acceptance of the mentor as a valuable resource is based on a realistic assumption—there is an important *maturational* and *competency* difference between them, or how is the mentor qualified to be the educator? The adult educator is more knowledgeable and experienced that the adult learner. In anticipating that benefits will flow from the mentor's expertise, the mentee's awareness of a superior-subordinate relationship is not only an accurate appraisal of the mentoring situation, but also the rationale for the mentee's willing participation *as the learner*. Though the mentor may certainly benefit as an adult learner from interaction with the mentee and may derive great personal satisfaction from providing valued assistance, the mentee legitimately invests in mentoring primarily as the recipient of assistance, not the provider.

The mentor's shared experiences should therefore reflect like helpful beams of lights on the mentee's pathway, not too diffuse and indirectly away from, nor too overly intense and directly into, the eyes of the mentee.

POSITIVE BELIEF IN ABILITY OF MENTEE

Clearly, the mentor's overall interpersonal style with the mentee—even when confrontive—would be described as *behaviorally positive*. However, the mentor's typically affirmative approach could become problematic if there are genuine concerns about the mentee's capability or reasonable probability of success in chosen educational, training, or career pursuits. For instance, mentors must realize, as committed as they may be assisting mentees, that they do not personally predetermine the maximum height of the cross-bar of potential in establishing how high mentees can leap. Many personal and situational variables influence the success of any individual mentee's journey into academic or career self-exploration. Mentors act as influences by assisting mentees to uncover, and to develop, their own unique combinations of interests, abilities, talents, and aptitudes.

Certainly, an important assumption of mentoring is that the mentor will offer the mentee, as an adult learner, a continuing empathetic foundation of positive psychological and emotional support, as well as legitimate encouragement based on a factual, realistic, and competency-based assessment of mentee attainments. The mentor's unmistakable belief in talent development should not, however, in any way lead to a "rose-colored glasses" type of feedback which inadvertently misleads the mentee by offering what is essentially false reassurance. The mentor's complex task is twofold: to motivate the mentee to maximize all available potential and opportunity while also, at the right time, to reference the real world of empirical evidence as the tangible marker of the mentee's progress in achieving educational, training, and career development goals.

Some of this feedback—the positive—will be welcomed by the mentee because it is clearly and accurately an affirmative assessment, and some of this feedback—the critical—may not be welcomed, even though it is just as factually accurate.

CONFIDENT VIEW OF RISK TAKING

The spectrum of usual mentee developmental areas—personal, educational, training, and career—will provide many opportunities for growth which do not appear particularly risky to either the mentee or mentor. In encouraging the mentee to devote personal time and energy to task performance, and to make the maximum use of all available resources in the pursuit of attainable goals, the mentor certainly should not imply that most activities must be approached as containing some potentially hidden or especially noteworthy risk.

Sometimes, though, the risk is real, with potentially serious repercussions to personal self-worth as well as to academic and career plans. Mentors will therefore want to initiate dialogues with mentees that encourage them to take a positive view of intelligent risks by weighing the real-world consequences—the advantages and disadvantages of each decision—as well as to realistically assess their commitment and readiness to handle the anticipated work and stress involved in each challenge. As an illustration of a basic and reasonably concrete approach, the mentor can introduce the cost/benefit idea of analyzing and resolving problems, and work with the mentee to formulate a written list of possible costs to the mentee as well as benefits which could be the result of particular courses of action (or inaction). The mentor's own shared experience in handling similar issues will often serve as a valuable source of motivation as well as pragmatic guidance for a mentee.

The responsibility for initiating any action containing risk must remain within the decision-making authority of the mentee, who as an independent adult learner, after reviewing the options, is understood to be operating in the world based on personal choice and not undue mentor influence. The balance between the mentor's sharing of personal experiences, advice, and recommendations, and the mentee's use of this information to make a more informed decision, may need to be explicitly clarified. Some mentees may not always recognize the often fine-line distinction between information as suggested guidance and information as implied strong advice or even command.

Mentees should be actively encouraged to express their ideas, beliefs, thoughts, and emotions regarding their decisions. They may even need to be directly asked to explain *why* they view a particular decision—which includes some risk—as in their own best interests.

ENCOURAGEMENT OF PERSONAL ACTION

The process of collaborative interaction with mentees will normally allow mentors to contribute in some meaningful way to goal clarification as well as to short-term and long-term planning. By expecting the mentee to make personal choices, the mentor will also be raising the issue of mentee responsibility for follow-through because the mentee must turn plans into the detailed actions necessary to accomplish educational and career objectives. In engaging in action-oriented dialogue, however, the mentor must be careful about ensuring that the mentee always retains personal autonomy for decisions.

To promote the reality of mentee independence, the mentor may need to emphasize that the mentee is not viewed as an object who is being acted upon, but instead, is appreciated as a valued and significant individual who is capable of intelligent, self-reflective, and independent choices. Moreover, the mentor may need to specifically indicate that the mentee is viewed as an adult learner who will emerge from collaborative mentor-mentee interaction and make personal decisions, choose actions, and accept responsibility for the results.

In exploring this dimension of mentoring, the mentor does not need to assume that every event involves reacting as if the existential weight of the world has been placed on the mentee's shoulders. Mentees will clearly differ in their maturity as well as in their ability to handle different issues. The mentor must remember that the uniqueness of each mentoring relationship will be a highly relevant factor in considering the helpful extent of mentor-initiated involvement to assist a particular mentee.

Also, the mentor will have varying amounts of direct connection to the operational phase of the mentee's education in the world external to the mentoring relationship. Important learning for the mentee will often involve performing observable tasks and receiving evaluations based on objective feedback directly offered to the mentee by influences other than the mentor, such as teachers and supervisors. In fact, most of the mentee's learning activities may occur outside the interpersonal territory of the individual mentoring sessions. The mentor may often be commenting on mentee actions which are actually based on the mentee's *self-reports* as an adult learner, and not on direct mentor observations. Mentees will not only differ in their empirical ability to handle different problems, but they also will differ in their ability to provide reliable self-assessments of their success. The mentor will therefore be faced with the problem of arriving at reasonable conclusions about the mentee's progress in the world-at-large based largely on information provided within the mentoring relationship.

Mentors also openly encourage mentees to engage in strategies and behaviors required for the achievement of mentee goals. By actively motivating the mentee to experience "here and now" opportunities in the world outside of the mentoring sessions, the mentor may sometimes inadvertently push the mentee to directly pursue immediate personal actions. The mentor must therefore be careful not only to explore the realistic options available to the mentee but also to review the implications of those decisions on the mentee.

The mentor's selectively shared experiences should convey a larger message that the mentee can carry from the present into the future—the lesson that sustained personal commitment is an essential motivational force which transforms personal decisions into achievable, tangible, real-world events. Often, the mentee will greatly profit from the mentor's personal experience by learning about the necessity of self-generating sustainability as a vital component of lifelong development. This type of collaborative dialogue, however, when centered around personal motivational issues relevant to present difficulties, or of anticipated problems when the mentee deals with future situations alone, could quite naturally cause other concerns to surface within the mentoring exchange.

As an illustration, there is clearly a prevalent view of contemporary adult learners as primary initiators, which essentially places them at the center of their own learning activities. The widely accepted "learning by doing" and "student-centered teaching" concepts have often become the norms of practice as a result of this general conceptual approach. Usually this direct participation model stresses progress and competency assessment based on observable performance by a professional evaluator of the learned behaviors. Unfortunately, this important guiding principle of active learning may be misinterpreted by some mentees who actually perceive adult development as more concerned with learning external to the self.

Even though the self-reflection model of learning has also been advocated as an integral aspect of adult education, some mentees may not really understand how genuine understanding is acquired from the apparent inaction of discussion or provided by the passive internal realities of more clearly introspective pathways to educational and career development. For action-oriented mentees who indicate impatience with the reflective dialogue style of mentoring, and primarily associate learning with real-world activity, mentors may need to reinforce the view that mentoring exchanges are also actions in the sense that the dialogues of cognitive analysis and planning involve exercise of the intellect to arrive at decisions.

Mentors may even need to emphasize that this thinking-through component of the problem-solution process should not merely be viewed as an overly cautious preliminary waiting period that unnecessarily slows down the ability to charge in the direction of the desirable, observable event. For instance, a mentor may personally agree that "think before you act, then definitely act" may be sound advice, and even be convinced that this point has also been absorbed by mentees as part of their inherited proverbial wisdom. But such an opinion may also turn out to be more of an assumption than a fact, and the point may therefore need to be explicitly examined.

SUMMARY

Mentor-mentee collaboration can range across a wide spectrum of topics and competencies and should serve to promote learning occurring inside, as well as external to, the mentoring relationship. Within the mentor model function, the mentor's involvement with mentee learning will primarily be as an influence who enhances the mentee's motivation to develop in academic, training, or career areas. Attention to the mentee's continuing progress toward selected goals, whether as a result of learning with others or alone, or as part of a formal and structured or informal and unstructured environment, is an essential aspect of the mentor model contribution to mentee development.

Some mentees may need guidance in adapting to the variety of human and technological resources now available. They may need considerable assistance as well to transcend their own particular learning styles so they can benefit from a diversity of opportunities, and not simply rely on approaches to learning that appear compatible with their own current preferences. Figure 7.1 contains a summary of the general strategy the mentor should consider when relying on shared personal experience as the method of integrating mentor model behaviors into the mentoring relationship.

Mentor Model

Shares life experiences and feelings as a "role model" with mentees in order to personalize and enrich the relationship

Purpose

To motivate mentees to take necessary risks, to make decisions and take actions without certainty of successful results, and to overcome difficulties in the journey toward educational and career goals

Mentor Behaviors

* Offer personal thoughts and genuine feelings to emphasize the value of learning from unsuccessful or difficult experiences (as trial-and-error and self-correction, and not as growth-limiting "failures").
* Select related examples from own life (and experiences as mentor of other mentees) based on probable motivational value.
* Provide a direct, realistic assessment of positive belief in mentee's ability to pursue attainable goals.
* Express a confident view of appropriate risk taking as necessary for personal, educational, training, and career development.
* Make statements that clearly encourage personal mentee actions to attain stated objectives.

Figure 7.1 Summary of mentor model function of mentor role.

CHAPTER 8

Pursuing the Dream

During the evolving mentoring relationship, the mentor and mentee will mutually formulate the plans necessary for achieving the mentee's expressed educational and professional goals. Dreams will be translated into task-related details as the mentor and mentee increasingly focus on those present-centered activities required for the attainment of objectives. The mentor, as an active participant in the ongoing assessment of the mentee's progress, at some point will also need to more specifically consider events beyond the press of immediate situational realities.

In fulfilling the responsibilities of the mentee vision function, the mentors should introduce a clear *future* orientation, and openly reference the fact that the mentees will transition to limited direct assistance from the mentor. Mentors will also need to stimulate mentees' critical thinking to include advance planning aimed at identifying other sources of assistance that might be available for them as adult learners. Potentially available as well as currently utilized resources could be reviewed as part of planning the mentees' continuing journey, but with a clear shift away from reliance on the mentors.

Although mentees will certainly differ in their preparation and competency in handling life's educational and career challenges, mentors should stress the continuing importance of three main points to mentees as adult learners:

1. Initiating decisions and actions

2. Actively managing personal changes and transitions

3. Confidently negotiating through educational, workplace, and life events

In addition, the mentor will need to focus more on the conscious connection between present-centered mutual mentor and mentee interaction and the future of the mentee's learning beyond the mentoring relationship. This aspect will assume more relevance as the mentee prepares to travel less and less in the company of the mentor.

Longer-term developmental issues will now receive increasing emphasis, even though the reality of fulfilling current task requirements still remains an important concern. At this point in the mentoring relationship, the amount of time and the frequency of mentoring sessions may even reflect a mutually phased-down schedule of interaction. Although the mentee's journey is still very much underway, the mentor's role as a *transitional figure* will now become much more apparent.

In attempting to incorporate behaviors relevant to the mentee vision function into the mentoring relationship, the mentor can use the following seven techniques:

1. Make statements which require reflection on present and future educational, training, and career attainments.

2. Ask questions aimed at clarifying perceptions (positive and negative) about personal ability to manage change.

3. Review individual choices based on a reasonable assessment of options and resources.

4. Make comments directed at analysis of problem-solving and decision-making strategies.

5. Express confidence in carefully thought-out decisions.

6. Offer remarks that show respect for mentees' capacity to determine their own future.

7. Encourage mentees to develop talents and pursue dreams.

REFLECTION ON PRESENT AND FUTURE ATTAINMENTS

Once, the historical record of the recent past indicated a reasonably slow progression of incremental change. But now, prior

sensible assumptions are risky as certain guides for predicting
the specific educational credentials and career competencies which
will be essential in the future. Certainly, the majority of mentors
and mentees have already been confronted by the reality that rapidly accelerating changes in the world make even the not-too-distant past an uncertain model for the impending future. The information highway metaphor now being used to describe the next
important stage of interaction between people and technology
represents another powerful signal of the profound impact such
change is anticipated to have on influencing essential aspects of
our society.

For the mentor to help the mentee become a proactive plan-
ner, a foundation premise underlying the adult education model of
learning—that of the adult as a *lifelong learner*—will need to be
accepted in principle and adopted as practice by the mentee. The
mentor, to illustrate the point, should highlight the critical theme
that a mature response to inevitable change now includes the assumption that continuous development be viewed as a rational behavior rather than as an exercise in educational or career crisis management. In addition, the mentor may need to carefully explain
that there are understandable reasons for the often unconscious
and anxiety-based resistance to even those changes which are initially perceived as probably beneficial (Charlesworth & Nathan,
1982). Some mentees will genuinely accept the stimulating, though
stressful, challenge of moving beyond the limits of individual comfort zones to further explore the educational and career implications and demands of change. Other mentees will acknowledge the
idea of change as a relevant general concern but not really process
"why" and "how" it may be an important and specific personal issue
for them as continuing adult learners.

The mentor should consider the mentee vision aspect of mentoring as assisting mentees to more perceptively anticipate their
future needs. If a mentee's current mode of decision making appears vulnerable to the twin problems of perceptual selection
and distortion, the mentor should carefully raise these as issues
because they are highly relevant examples of self-defeating behaviors. Uncorrected, such mentee blocks will no only prevent present
adaptive skills from developing, they will also limit the mentee's capacity to actively and reasonably project into areas of per-

sonal, educational, and career growth that may be required in the future.

The mentor may need to initiate a review of the mentee's more emotionally comfortable, more intellectually stable versions and truisms of the past that have been accepted as unquestioned realities and which now form the basis of much mentee belief and perception. Mentees should be asked to examine the merit of the concerns still posed by astute futurist thinkers about the risks of complacency, and to consider if, by fixating too exclusively on the past and present as the prototype, they as adult learners are now perhaps engaged in building an *obsolete* model of their own educational, training, and career future.

The reasoned and prudent forecasting offered by today's respected futurists appears to be based on a powerful and provocative idea—that any sound, factually based, and sustainable understanding of contemporary and future reality must acknowledge the profound implications raised by the speed and depth of change increasingly characteristic of this century. Planning for even the near future is therefore now viewed as including, as a major component of relevant preparation, the development of an individual's capability to adapt to increasing acceleration in all fields (Naisbitt & Aburdene, 1990; Peters, 1987). The growing concern of educators and trainers in both academia and business is the vigorous advocacy of constant preparation as the means by which adults will acquire and maintain the competencies required to successfully adapt to constant change.

The behavioral profile of the productive adult in the not-too-distant future matches the attributes of the ideal self-initiating, self-directed continuing adult learner long proposed by the adult education movement (Marsick, 1987; Merriam & Cunningham, 1989). And some mentors will discover mentees who already share the belief that flexible behavior is truly a requirement for effective functioning in our changing world. Of course, mentees will vary in their own maturity with respect to possessing the quality of adaptability as a competency. The mentor must differentiate between mentees who presently demonstrate behaviorally flexible responses to real-world demands, and those mentees who cognitively understand but are still struggling to practice what they profess.

In commenting on the relevance of past mentee experiences, the mentor may therefore need to frequently highlight a particularly contemporary point: Rapid and continuous change requires that the mentee anticipate, develop, and self-monitor the educational and career competencies necessary for a meaningful life.

PERCEPTIONS ABOUT MANAGING CHANGE

Mentors will ask questions designed to clarify mentee perceptions about their abilities as adult learners to manage change. Mentees will respond by offering both positive and negative examples as their own personal reference points. Some mentees may comment that the mentor is preaching a paradox by predicting that "uncertainty is certain." However, the majority of mentees will be ready to learn how to acquire adaptive behaviors. They need little convincing that adaptability is a foundation survival skill.

The mentor should therefore introduce adaptability as a component of general planning. In addressing this, the mentor must be careful not to overdramatize the point or to aggressively indicate that any mentee unable to face this challenge of adaptive competency will just float along, enduring a rather pathetic life and existing only as an acted-upon individual.

In processing this type of information, some mentees may require substantial encouragement and explanation. An understandable initial response to the reality of profound change is often a stress overreaction. This is especially true for the mentee who relies on models of past success, which were obtained in a simpler and slower-speed world, as *the* predictor of continued success in a much altered environment. The demands of change for many mentees quite normally will raise important concerns and anxieties about their personal abilities to transfer competencies developed in the past to the projected future. Sometimes the issues raised by such dialogue may also cause adult learners to question their own capability to maintain the control required to adapt and survive in the changed academic and workplace landscape.

By examining mentee expectations of achievement, mentors

can help them clarify the extent to which they visualize themselves as capable of educational and career success. If mentees indicate that they are experiencing change as a destabilizing force, and as a strongly felt forfeiture of ability to exert reasonable control over personal decisions, the mentor should offer sensitive support focused on restoring the mentee's loss of self-confidence.

As a logical and corrective counterbalance to the weight of prior mentee negative experiences or overly anxious responses, the mentor can advocate the proactive approach to learning, which asserts that strategies for management of the self in a changing environment can be developed reasonably well. Specific mentee reactions will vary along a continuum from the passive "I'm lucky if I survive" to the naive "My willpower alone will conquer all." Mentors should therefore be prepared to explore in some depth the mentee's ideas on this important topic. The mentor's objective will be to help the mentee to develop a healthy and sustainable personal vision of the not-too-distant future as an exciting, perhaps even demanding world, but not as an overwhelming or frightening place to live.

Although mentors will need to acknowledge that individuals cannot control all life events, they can also advocate the power of *responsible influence*—if preparation and action can make any reasonable difference in a particular outcome, then such an opportunity will be recognized and acted upon by the mentee, and not just lost in a fog of inaction. This positive view of change should help anchor the mentee's belief in a realistic commitment to the hard work associated with educational and career achievement. It should also reinforce the important point that there is an earned pleasure derived from the effort to achieve, not simply from the result.

REVIEW OF MENTEE CHOICES

A mentor may need to review the mentee's future-orientated goals by undertaking a pragmatic assessment of the options that were considered and the resources which were used as the basis for decisions. Certainly, the mentor and mentee will already have spent considerable time in planning and evaluating the mentee's actions and performance in the pursuit of stated objectives. The intention of this additional review is not to reexamine familiar territory, but rather to connect the present with the future by considering the mentee's readiness to transition from one set of assumptions to another if events significantly alter a mentee's personal situation. The particular focus of the dialogue is on illustrating and reinforcing the need for flexibility.

In reviewing the mentee's options and resources, the mentor should factually approach both the mentee's *organizational options*, which are connected to such realities as credentials, training, and career-relevant experience within the educational and work environment, and the resources within the individual's *personal network* of other support, which usually involves the social context of family, friends, and community. The mentor's goal is to ensure, as much as possible, that the mentee maintains a balanced and rational response to change by avoiding extreme reactions if the unexpected occurs and different choices are warranted.

This review and monitoring of available options and resources may require that a mentee's present world be considered again as a source of useful situations for learning, even though the focus is primarily on future application. For example, a mentee who has generally benefited from the mentoring experience, but who still could profit by understanding more about how to properly maneuver within the educational or workplace system to obtain legitimate assistance, could be encouraged to undertake additional tasks as on-the-job-training under the guidance of the mentor.

ANALYSIS OF STRATEGIES

The mentor and mentee will have engaged in considerable dialogue by working through the problem-solving/decision-making process The mentor's point in analyzing the strategies involved should now focus less on the mechanics of the approach and more on the quality of critical thinking revealed by the mentee. The mentor should assess the mentee's ability to analyze the significance of the factual material being filtered, which involves personally connecting the meaning of the *objective* data to the plans of the *subjective* mentee in a sensible and thoughtful way.

Based on previous experience in the mentoring relationship, a mentor will have formed an opinion about the mentee's handling of problems. Some mentees demonstrate a general competency while others vary in their ability to deal effectively with separate parts of the decision process. In preparing the mentee to project the use of a problem-solving model into the future as a workable approach, the mentor should address the mentee's recent situation— what are the results of the mentee's decisions, and how have such choices best served this unique mentee in the present?

References selected from current examples of productive mentee decisions can become a guide to anticipate areas of general strength in future actions. A review of the mentee's vulnerabilities, as revealed by instances of unproductive decisions, will assist in identifying those areas of relative weakness which need strengthening to become future competencies. The mentor, with the mentee's active participation, can examine how well the mentee has paid attention to collecting data by using the following criteria: (1) adequate detailing of information, (1) reliability of sources, (3) realistic appraisal of educational and career options, and (4) genuine sense of personal commitment to the tasks involved in reaching goals.

The central message for the mentee is that the lessons learned from living can provide hard won but valuable knowledge, which can be transferred into increased competency as a problem solver, if the mentee reflects upon, consciously learns from, and incorporates the relevant meaning derived from the experience into future actions. The mentor's importance as an influence will be to convey a belief in the same continuing commitment to carefully reasoned analysis and pragmatic application, so that the mentee can travel beyond the mentoring relationship into the future, as a confident, self-reliant adult learner.

EXPRESSIONS OF CONFIDENCE IN DECISIONS

The mentor must acknowledge and reinforce the autonomy of the mentee as a capable adult learner. Expressing confidence in a mentee's ability to act on, and if necessary, self-correct decisions is essential, because an assumption of mentoring-as-learning is that errors in judgment will occur, even with a mentor's assistance. The mentor therefore presumes that the mentee will learn by assuming responsibility and accountability for independent actions, whether the results are positive or negative.

The importance of a respectful and confident approach to mentee potential, however, is not meant to imply that the mentor must present a false or nonassertive persona when there clearly are very different views. A mentor may certainly confront a mentee, if warranted, and provide direct feedback to help the mentee examine clear discrepancies in fact, logic, or performance. In this instance, the mentor may be treading a difficult path, that of exploring the extent to which a mentee's already demonstrated current competency is commensurate with any reasonable probability of continuing future success. Without demeaning the mentee, the mentor will need to communicate any genuine reservations about the mentee's preparation or achieved competency when there could be a possibility of serious consequences.

Also, if a lack of positive results is anticipated by the mentor, and the mentee proceeds by considering but not accepting the mentor's present views, then the mentor may fairly assume that learning by disappointment will also provide another important lesson—that most errors can be corrected and most risk is not life threatening. If the expected failure does occur during the mentoring relationship, then the mentor should be fully prepared to use the event as a positive opportunity to encourage the mentee to learn from mistakes.

By taking a clear-headed but nonjudgmental (not an "I told you so") approach, the mentor can participate with the mentee in a calm review of previous plans, strategies, actions, and performance. The emphasis on meaningful learning in the "here-and-now" should then shift to the important "next time" reality of mentee performance so that the value of continued learning—of the transfer of learning from one situation to another—is fully understood and practiced.

If the anticipated failure does not happen, or does but with less serious consequences to the mentee than predicted, the mentee may well have an opportunity to relearn another lesson—

that even the most well-intentioned and thoughtful mentor's advice should be viewed as an *option*. The mentor's consistent message is that the mentee must finally choose from among the available options and accept the individual consequences—positive or not. The mentee cannot later refer to the choice of a specific option as somehow a mentor command in order to relieve the mentee from personal responsibility.

Belief in the future starts in the present. Ideally, the mentor as a seasoned and mature role model who responds to risk taking as an important chance to learn, will provide a direct and healthy reference point for future mentee decisions and actions. Most mentees will profit from this positive model of using experience as an opportunity for self-correctable learning. They will be less likely to be blocked by a self-limiting fear of mistakes the next time.

RESPECT FOR CAPACITY TO
DETERMINE FUTURE

Mentors demonstrate confidence in mentees by their interpersonal behaviors toward them. From the beginning of the mentoring relationship, a significant source of this belief is communicated by the mentor's realistic but not patronizing respect for the mentee's ability to positively function as a continuing learner in the ongoing pursuit of educational and career goals. The mentor needs to express an acceptance of the mentee's capacity—the communicated recognition of the adult learner as capable of benefiting from trial-and-error learning—especially if clearly different positions exist between them about which path to follow. This sends an important and specific signal of respect about the mentee's positive potential to develop as a learner beyond the assistance of the mentor. A belief in the mentee which is grounded in the very foundation of the mentoring relationship thus enables the mentor to express respect for the reasonable capacity of the mentee to function actively in the present and thereby to influence the future.

On the mentee's journey, the mentor walks only part of the

way. In reflecting upon the future value of mentoring for an individual mentee, a mentor can consider a simple but workable guiding principle: If a mentee is reasonably receptive, and a mentor is reasonably proficient, the mentoring relationship will most likely be a beneficial learning experience. Most competent mentors will provide at least some meaningful, tangible assistance to most mentees just by communicating a continuing faith in their potential.

How much positive difference the mentor's involvement makes at the time or in the future remains difficult to quantify. But many of those fortunate enough to have experienced meaningful mentoring vividly recall the mentor's powerful belief in their developmental capacity as a vital source of inspiration (Daloz, 1986). Such genuine personal support appears to resonate through mentoring relationships and to create relevant and memorable learning for mentees.

ENCOURAGEMENT TO PURSUE DREAMS

The mentee often enters the mentoring relationship with a dream, or develops one as a result, and the mentee exits with a dream as well. Some of the time, between the formulation and the attainment of a personal dream, is spent in the company of a mentor. Mentoring time is therefore primarily that of readiness—of increasing competencies, of skills assessment, of renewed motivation and commitment, and of general preparation to continue as an independent adult learner.

Certainly, the alert mentor will be aware of *how* far the mentee has already journeyed, *what* needs attention now to assist the mentee's development during the mentoring relationship, and *why* the mentee should address certain concerns in the present relevant to the future. In some instances, the mentee's dream, or an important component of it, will be realized while the mentor and mentee are still involved in mentoring activities. The mentor's direct contribution may therefore be nearly completed, and depending on the status of the relationship, the contact between mentor and mentee may soon dissolve. This conclusion should be viewed as an honorable resolution for both the mentor and the mentee of their mutual commitment.

The mentor and mentee must remember that an important assumption of mentoring is that a long-term friendship is *not* a direct goal of a mentoring relationship. Less and less contact should not be interpreted as diminishing the value of the previous mentoring relationship. In fact, more separation may be viewed as a natural ending to a relationship which was always about the increasingly independence of the mentee. If friendship has occurred, and this type of more equal relational involvement continues beyond the mentoring experience, then such an event can be accepted as an unexpected but welcomed benefit. And the same mentee, while maintaining this friendship, may continue to dream, to pursue dreams, and to realize dreams, but not necessarily with significant input from the prior mentor. The obvious encouragement of the mentor has now been transformed into a subtle influence, as former mentees continue their independent and self-directed talent development in educational, training, and career pursuits.

SUMMARY

Table 8.1 provides a summary of those mentor-initiated behaviors which promote the mentee vision function. The content of these mentor and mentee discussions is clearly applicable to the later stages of mentoring interaction, especially to topics with a future orientation beyond the domain of the current mentoring relationship. However, such concerns are not necessarily raised only in the later phases of the mentoring relationship. The mentee is on an extended individual journey, and the mentee's personal ability to manage change at any point, and to center in the present while anticipating the future, is always an appropriate subject of mentor-mentee dialogue.

Mentee Vision

Stimulates mentees' critical thinking with regard to envisioning their own future and developing their personal and professional potential

Purpose

To encourage mentees as they manage personal changes and take initiatives in their transitions through life events as independent adult learners

Mentor Behaviors

* Make statements which require reflection on present and future educational, training, and career attainments.
* Ask questions aimed at clarifying perceptions (positive and negative) about personal ability to manage change.
* Review individual choices based on a reasonable assessment of options and resources.
* Make comments directed at analysis of problem-solving and decision-making strategies.
* Express confidence in carefully thought-out decisions.
* Offer remarks that show respect for mentees' capacity to determine their own future.
* Encourage mentees to develop talents and pursue dreams.

Figure 8.1 Summary of mentee vision function of mentor role.

CHAPTER 9

Planning and Operating the Program

This work has proposed a model of learning which uses the behavioral role of the mentor as the primary guide to understanding what makes mentor-mentee interaction an adult mentoring relationship. This model also presents the mentees as responsible for assuming a significant degree of personal involvement as participant adult learners in their own developmental journey. The clear emphasis on mentor behavior is not intended to minimize the accountability of the mentee as a learner, but rather to maximize the contribution of the mentor as a vital participant in the learning process—to highlight what the mentor does as an influence.

Given the importance associated with the behavioral profile of the proficient mentor, those responsible for planning the organizationally sponsored mentoring program should certainly include a relevant mentor orientation component, as well as continuing training seminars to assist individuals in improving their competency in the art of mentoring. The focus of these opportunities for learning should be on enhancing the ability of mentors to form collaborative interpersonal relationships that truly assist mentees in developing their intellectual, affective, and career potential.

The early seminars for the mentors need to address selected issues of particular relevance in a mentoring relationship, such as mentor authority over the mentee, gender, ethnicity, and age. These topics should be introduced to clarify their possible impact on the evolving interpersonal interaction between the mentor and the mentee. The objective would be to increase the mentors' knowledge and awareness so they can initiate and respond with effective strategies if possible issues, such as promotion and evaluation authority, become real problems. Differences between the mentor and the mentee should also be explored as valuable sources of mutually respectful learning rather than as barriers to be overcome.

Planning for the mentees should also be approached with the idea of providing early positive experiences for learning as an integral part of the program. There should be an emphasis on the sensitive handling of their initial recruitment and orientation, as well as provision for the organized availability of program resources, such as follow-up group seminars and private consultations with program coordinators to discuss individual concerns. For mentees, this supplemental dimension will enrich the reality of their face-to-face involvement with mentors.

While the overall mentoring relationship may appear to unfold as a series of naturally occurring events, those responsible for creating and nurturing it will need to invest a good deal of energy, especially in the beginning stages, to ensure that all possible effort is channeled into constructive contact between mentors and mentees. The planning and operating of the sponsored mentoring program will now be covered in more detail, based primarily on expanding the points which have been recommended for enhancing mentor-mentee participation.

PROACTIVE MENTORING PROGRAMS

By actively initiating the establishment of an official mentoring program, organizations have already taken a major step. Overall institutional goals will guide the general development and operation of the program, but in the preliminary stages four significant concerns must be addressed:

1. The recruitment and orientation of mentees

2. The recruitment and orientation/training of mentors

3. The time committed to the development of the relationship

4. The matching of mentors and mentees

Each of these topics will now be examined.

Recruitment of Mentees

The early need for a proactive approach to attracting mentee candidates may not always be obvious. Simply advertising the availability of mentors and then assuming that mentees will immediately respond may often be unrealistic. In fact, those adult learners and employees who could benefit the most may also be the least assertive about personally seeking out a mentor. Many avenues should be used to directly contact and encourage participation by all potential mentees, from mailings, to recruitment sessions attended by mentee-peers who have already experienced mentoring, to small group orientation meetings between mentors and potential mentees.

Sometimes, the more "high risk" individuals who did not initially respond to the invitation to be mentored can be identified by their marginal performance as indicated by academic transcripts in education or job appraisals in the workplace. By contrast, some people who technically are quite competent may need assistance not because they lack academic or work-related skills, but because of their personal and professional "invisibility," withdrawal, and poor social adaptation. The representatives of the organization who use this type of information to locate and then refer adult learners or employees as candidates for mentoring will, of course, need to be sure that the sources used to identify such individuals do not violate any confidentiality (legal) prohibitions.

In addition, while some people will quickly welcome the overture of assistance, others may retreat into anger and denial even if compassionately and patiently approached. The persons doing the contacting will need to be well prepared for and sensitive to the emotional responses of those who could feel very threatened about being viewed openly as inadequate performers, whether in terms of academics, job functions, or social skills. Noble intentions and genuine offers of assistance could quickly be turned into counterproductive responses if those being approached take flight rather than face the reality of their own negative visibility. To mitigate such reactions, intermediaries such as counselors, instructors, managers, and student or workplace peers can be part of the recruitment process, since they at least may not be viewed as strangers offering assistance based only on the cold review of records.

In establishing a mentoring program, a reasonable assumption is that most potential mentees will be initially unclear about the specific benefits of mentoring. The more assertive and savvy adult learners are more likely to be first in line to inquire about a mentor, while the less confident and the high risk must often be actively sought out and recruited if they also are to have the opportunity to become mentees.

Orientation for Mentees

As indicated above, the recruitment of mentees begins with a broad-based advertising campaign to explain the benefits of the mentoring relationship. After this phase, an orientation session should be scheduled, which can be conducted as two separate but connected meetings to avoid information overload and to allow proper time for discussion. Nine specific points will need to be clarified:

1. The matching of mentors and mentees

2. The scheduling and length of individual sessions

3. The overall timeframe of interaction

4. Reasonable topics and goals for discussion

5. Mutual activities to consider

6. Procedures regarding session notes/records and confidentiality

7. Expected commitment of the participants

8. Available third-party resources to help resolve problems or conflicts

9. Grounds for changing or terminating a mentor-mentee relationship

The orientation should highlight the stated objectives of the mentoring program. This approach helps to prevent mentee misperception or misunderstanding and promotes an important connection between reasonable mentee expectations and realistic mentor and program capabilities and resources. Mentees should be encouraged to ask questions about any aspect of program operation, and to express personal concerns they might have about any facet of the mentoring relationship. The handling of questions is particularly important because the early credibility of the program itself will be reflected in the honest, open, factual, and nonjudgmental answers offered by the first representatives of the organization with whom the mentees have any significant contact.

The mentees should also be offered basic guidelines relevant to preparing for the initial sessions with the mentors. For example, mentees should be encouraged to reflect on their own immediate and future personal, academic, and career goals, and to consider how mentors could assist them in planning strategies for achieving these objectives. Mentees should be specifically asked to think about and then to discuss with their mentors the skills, insight, support, and knowledge they as learners hope to acquire as a result of the mentoring experience. In addition, the importance of being on time and of keeping all appointments should be emphasized so that there will be no doubt that mentoring time is perceived as valuable.

Those conducting the orientations should encourage mentees as well as mentors to focus the early mentoring sessions on specific objectives because factually based topics of mutual interest can create a structure around which to center the mentor-mentee dialogue. Some mentees could construe the lack of an emerging or concrete agenda after a number of sessions as a "nothing is happening" problem.

To accelerate the learning curve in a positive way, the mentees, even in this preliminary stage of mentoring, should be asked to assume reasonable responsibility for identifying their own topics and activities for exploration. Such an approach will often prove productive because it will reinforce the important message that a supportive, collaborative, and goals-oriented developmental journey is underway, and that mentees, not just mentors, are expected to actively participate in the experience.

After the orientation, and when the actual mentor-mentee contacts begin to occur, several seminars conducted by a knowledgeable facilitator should be offered to the mentees as an early follow-up on their progress. This approach is especially valuable because a supportive and nonthreatening environment will encourage mentees to express themselves and thereby promote more stimulating interactions with their peers. In addition to the important general exchange of ideas, perceptions, and beliefs, mentees can also review their own situations, share concerns, offer suggestions, and learn about the specific activities of other mentoring pairs. Often, the items raised for discussion will include many of the nine points presented at the initial orientation, which now have the reality of specific mentor-mentee interaction.

At the seminars, mentees may understandably wish to use their own mentoring relationships as examples when they express their concerns regarding a variety of unmet personal expectations. Mentees may attempt to offer detailed reactions to mentors perceived as offering insufficient guidance or demonstrating inadequate interest. An essential guideline which must be stressed is that the purpose of these meetings is not to engage in negative ventilation, such as using the time to attack individual mentors if conflict has already occurred, or to criticize either the personality or the motives of specific people.

A clear illustration of a serious topic that should be discussed privately with a program coordinator, but not opened up to the mentee group as a personal problem in need of a group-sponsored solution, would be disruptive friction between a particular mentee and mentor that might result in termination of their relationship. Besides the real problem of disclosing what the mentor could consider to be the details of a private issue at a public forum, the mentee would also be indicating who the mentor in questions was, since the identities of the matched pairs are usually general information.

Seminar coordinators will therefore need to provide very clear direction, and sometimes even active intervention, to ensure that information disclosed within the mentee peer group is properly screened through the filter of astute and sensitive judgment. The focus of the group should be on exchanging views and constructively searching for and sharing creative ways of maximizing their mentoring experience. This concern, however, about discretion is not intended to suggest that facilitators sugarcoat difficult but legitimate issues which could be necessary topics of discussion.

A mentee, for instance, who believes that little actual mentoring is occurring, or who requests assistance to identify strategies for interacting more effectively with a mentor, has raised relevant concerns. But the feedback must be carefully aimed at considering positive mentee initiatives, rather than directed at criticism of the mentor or blame of the mentee for displaying an attitude problem. If these seminars are presented as a solutions-focused forum for the mentees, the negative tendency to worry about "Whose fault is it?" can be replaced with the positive reaction of "What can be done about it?"

The group approach to maximizing the learning opportunities provided by mentoring relationships can add a valuable dimension to the overall mentoring experience for the mentees.

Recruitment of Mentors

A variety of initiatives can be taken to advertise for mentors. If the program is already operational, current mentors can be asked to personally contact colleagues. The usual flyers, in-house publications, and print and electronic methods of communication are helpful. Raising the topic at a variety of the usual organizational meetings, with a spokesperson for the mentoring program briefly appearing on the agenda, can directly contact prospective mentors. In the formative stages, open and active support by those in senior positions will often help to attract participants by indicating that the organization is committed to the success of the program.

A guideline for establishing the overall content and tone of both the recruitment and the orientation/seminar components should be the assumption that persons considering the mentor role already have a genuine commitment to assisting others. They are interested in learning more about the purpose and value of the mentoring relationship and in acquiring the practical or applied knowledge relevant to proficiency in the mentor role.

Orientation and Continuing Seminars for Mentors

The orientation for mentors should begin with one session which focuses on providing basic information about the programmatic and behavioral facets of mentoring. Then two follow-up sessions should be immediately scheduled to orient mentors to their unique interpersonal role in the adult mentoring relationship. Although program coordinators and mentors may be able to coordinate attendance at a more extended model of orientation sessions, the proposed schedule of at least one general informational and two more specific orientation/preparation sessions is a reasonable minimum to launch the mentoring program.

Several continuing education style seminars should be scheduled soon after mentors and mentees start meeting. The purpose is to solicit from the mentors any concerns or topics they want to discuss, as well as any competencies they have identified for fine tuning. After several months, as the mentor-mentee relationships develop, a seminar can be held once every month to offer regular opportunities for the accumulation of valuable learning to be shared.

Content and Sequence of Sessions

The depth and range of topics, issues, and skills which can be realistically covered at the orientations and seminars will depend on the schedule: How much time and how many meetings will be devoted to mentoring? The following discussion should be used as a general guide because the reality of less or more allocated time will clearly affect the degree to which the orientations and seminars are superficial and highly compressed or substantive and comprehensive.

Generally, mentor preparation in the orientation sessions and early training seminars should be front loaded with practical guidance. Attention should be devoted to a review of the mentors' anticipated reactions as well as to their actual responses and concerns based on face-to-face contact with mentees. By helping them to meaningfully interpret self-assessment and feedback critiques at training seminars, mentors can learn to more objectively recognize their own emerging ability to function as skilled and significant influences in the lives of mentees. Such an analytical and supportive approach can assist mentors in developing confidence and competency. The training dimension and the mentoring relationship can thus become a more fulfilling experience for mentors.

At the main orientation and later seminars, a significant theme for program administrators to emphasize is that the mentoring relationship is valuable to the mentee as a source of personal, educational, and career learning for two essential reasons: (1) the *internal* value of the ongoing interpersonal dialogue, which derives from direct exchanges with the mentor, and (2) the *external* value of the relationship, which allows the mentee to benefit from the mentor's support and guidance while pursing activities outside of the sessions, such as self-directed study, short duration workshops, on-the-job-training programs, or formal training and college courses. Mentees therefore should be viewed as profiting from the *blend* of learning and of exploring many possibilities to develop their knowledge and proficiencies.

After the preliminary orientation, the two more in-depth orientation sessions, scheduled within several weeks of each other if possible, will introduce the specifics of mentoring. These linked sessions should present mentoring as an interactive and collaborative developmental process, examine the concept of the mentor role and six behavioral functions, and explain the idea of the phases aspect of the mentoring relationship. Other important concerns to address are the match, the handling of conflict, the use of mentor notes, and the focus on mentee goals to provide an early sense of structure to the dialogue.

The Principles of Adult Mentoring Scale can be distributed at the main orientation session, along with the comment that the instrument will be used as a reference for exploring the dynamics of the mentor-mentee experience, and not as a means for public examination of individual mentor scores. Also, concerns about a mentor being influenced in any way prior to completing the scale by explanations and discussions at the orientation (assuming the scale cannot be distributed before) should be explained as of less importance than the more significant use of the scale as a tool for providing a concentrated learning experience about mentoring. Scale scores reflect a point of departure, not of arrival.

Also, at the main orientation and follow-up sessions, two other essential points should be offered to highlight the central purpose of subsequent mentor preparation. First, those presenting the orientation should state that, in addition to mentor self-reflection based on use of the scale, feedback in the form of critiques will be available at the seminars to improve the abilities of professionals to perform as capable mentors. Such training will be conducted as a responsible and responsive program facilitated by individuals with relevant information and experience about mentoring adult learners.

Second, there should be a direct statement that respect for adults as learners will guide all seminar participation. Mentor training seminars beyond the initial orientation sessions will become increasingly personal, collaborative, and experiential. They must be based on mutual regard for acknowledged differences, exploration of options, and voluntary involvement in evaluation (both self and peer) to enhance the knowledge and improve the skills of the mentor. Mentors should also be informed that they will not be demeaned by being subjected to a psychology-by-the-numbers approach, in which the "right" way of handling mentees or situations is proposed. Their individual approaches will not be criticized as deviating from some rigidly correct formula.

Instead, mentors need to know that they will be viewed as professionals who are themselves adult learners interested in the creative opportunity to increase proficiency in the behavioral role of mentor. Such a message is consistent with the consideration they will need to show their mentees.

With regard to the content of the initial training, the early phase of the mentoring experience is a useful reference point around which to center the two linked orientation follow-up sessions and beginning seminars. A specific emphasis on the first and second actual mentor-mentee meetings will provide concrete guidance and an opportunity for a more in-depth question and answer forum. As an illustration, a valuable learning activity for the mentors (at seminars as well) is to have more and less experienced mentors briefly role play several mentoring interactions. The program facilitator can then engage the audience in an analysis of the mentor-mentee behaviors which were observed. Afterwards, all of the mentors can form into groups of three or four to allow each person to participate in role plays as mentor and mentee, and to contribute comments as objective observer. The guidelines suggested for reviewing mentor role functions can be used to assist in focusing the discussions and critiques (see Appendix C).

Before entering the arena of training, the coordinator of the orientations and seminars should explain that a variety of positive and appropriate strategies exists for mentors to draw on in their interactions with mentees. The objective of role simulations and mutual critiques must be understood as an effort to explore various approaches. It is not a way to transform another mentor into oneself because of the belief that only one approach is workable. If there is a difference of opinion, a mentor who takes a highly dogmatic position with another is essentially saying: "The problem with you is, you're not me!" Although mentors should certainly be encouraged to express firm and informed views, they should also be offered direct feedback when they appear to be simply defending fixed positions, or one of the benefits of the seminars—to broaden a mentor's repertoire of responses—will not be realized.

The coordinator should highlight another important point: A noticeable behavioral attitude often revealed early by successful mentors, and noticed in particular by mentees, is the mentor's openness, receptivity, and genuine concern for people and learning. While mentors certainly should not be painted as candidates for sainthood, they do need to recognize the vital importance of projecting an accepting attitude to the mentees. The power of these initial reactions to create an overall positive mentee response to the mentor should therefore be affirmed at the orientation as more than a merely superficial concern about first impressions.

In fact, the point should be stressed that some mentees will quickly recoil if they interpret an initially tough-sounding mentor demand (as in a stern lecture about "What I expect from you as your mentor!") as more suggestive of an impending judgmental and critical relationship than of a productive learning experience. Since the mentees are essentially in the more vulnerable position, such a response is not surprising, especially since a mentee's expectations will be keyed to the anticipated warmer reception of the proposed helping relationship.

Those responsible for orientations and seminars for new mentors should be tuned to the genuine concerns that some individuals express about not being counselors or psychologists. Coordinators should be alert as well to the quieter assumption by others of possessing innate behavioral proficiency for the mentor role, especially if such a view has not been in any way confirmed by relevant objective feedback or enhanced through appropriate preparation. In identifying the difference between assumed and realized behavioral competency, Hanson (1983) offers a noteworthy observation regarding the significance of training for the mentoring role:

> It is important to recognize that while many mentor-protege relationships occur naturally through a mutual selection process, many individuals are unfamiliar with the nature of mentoring relationships and do not understand what is entailed in being either a mentor or a protege. Thus, a recommendation of the study is that programs be developed to teach mentor as well as protege behaviors. These programs can help potential proteges and mentors learn how to develop beneficial mentoring relationships and how to avoid some of the potential hazards and pitfalls. Training programs such as these may be necessary in schools, communities, businesses and organizations, and higher education. (p. 232)

In reality, too often the selection of mentor candidates is approached with the emphasis on simply finding volunteers. Given the significance of the mentor's behavior, the issue of actual preparation for the role of mentor is of genuine importance. A proficient mentor will be better able to stimulate mutual creative energies, especially in the powerful first stage of mentoring, so that a positive relationship experience determines the direction of their evolving interaction.

But what backgrounds do most people bring to adult mentoring? This is an important consideration, especially since the fact of one-to-one interaction occurring as an event will not itself spontaneously produce a meaningful mentoring relationship. As suggested by many reports, both educators and managers recruited as mentors generally derive their view of themselves as influences in the lives of students or employees *primarily* from their experience in group interactions (Civikly, 1986). Numerous studies also imply (Schlossberg, Lynch, & Chickering, 1989) that the classroom or group managerial reference point for many faculty and managers is too often an uncritcal and unexamined domain of assumed professional competence, with limited opportunities for critical and reflective feedback offered to the person acting in the instructional or managerial role.

Given this general context, then what preparation and experience are individuals specifically transferring as they transition into the intensely personal world of one-to-one interaction between the mentor and the adult learner? And what specific behavioral baseline of professional competencies are prospective mentors referencing as the model for the mentor role?

Mentoring Adult Learners has approached the mentoring relationship from the perspective of the mentor as a professional functioning in an organizationally sponsored program. But whether primarily associated with education, business, or government, the effective mentor has been portrayed as capable of demonstrating mentoring skills in six related categories of behavior in the complete mentor role: Relationship Emphasis, Information Emphasis, Facilitative Focus, Confrontive Focus, Mentor Model, and Mentee Vision. These mentor competencies have also been presented as directly influencing the quality of the mentoring experience for the mentee.

The model of the complete mentor role proposed in this book can provide a number of immediate options as a guide to assist mentors in the development of their mentoring skills. For example, mentors could begin by privately reviewing their relative effectiveness or ineffectiveness as revealed by the profile in the Principles of Adult Mentoring Scale profile. The mentors could then use this information as a source to recommend specific topics for seminars in which they would like to participate, based on their perception of their individual learning needs.

In addition, by using the explanation of mentor functions (see Appendix C) as a guideline for continuing self-evaluation, the mentors could monitor their own progress in the real world of mentoring interaction, and then return to share insights at the seminars based on the results of their self-appraisals. Such direct input could also serve as a valuable reservoir of strategies and themes for future training seminars.

Program administrators could use the model of the complete mentor role as a basis for surveying the mentor group as a whole, in an attempt to identify patterns of perceived effectiveness or ineffectiveness. The goal at the seminars would be to use such information as a means of engaging mentors in a nonthreatening competency review. Often, this reality *check* is especially helpful because some mentors may overestimate or underestimate their contribution to the mentoring relationship. Many of the scale item statements could be used as a reference to examine in more detail the shared ideas and experiences regarding the content dimension of mentor-mentor dialogue. This could include a wide range of topics relevant to educational and career concerns.

Two other factors will require consideration as extremely relevant influences on the probable value of the mentoring experience: (1) the length and (2) the frequency of mentoring sessions. Although these issues appear related more to the mechanics than to the substance of mentoring, both time factors have a substantial impact of the quality of the mentoring experience for the mentee. The following will provide the basic information necessary for presentation and discussion at the main orientation for mentors.

Length of Sessions

While the actual qualitative significance of a mentoring relationship cannot be assured by a simple clocktime measurement, the issue of what constitutes a reasonable amount of time spent together remains an important concern. Considering the objectives of mentoring, mentors and mentees will obviously need to allow sufficient time for the relationship dimension to develop and for the necessary information to be collected, explored, and applied as decisions and actions.

For a mentoring relationship to flourish, the mentor needs to establish and maintain the six functions of the complete mentor role. The mentor and mentee should consider sessions which average 30–45 minutes, especially in the early stages of the relationship. One of the assumptions of mentoring is that adequate time will be devoted for the usual processes of interpersonal interaction to occur so that people who sometimes begin as strangers can gradually develop a meaningful mentoring relationship. Much less time together may not be a realistic approach if meaningful interpersonal interaction is to occur in the critical relational and informational dimensions between the mentor and the mentee—which are the tasks of the early phases of mentoring.

Mentoring is time consuming because it is a gradual rather than a quick process. The time is often spent, not on following a neat and clean straight-line road toward goals, but on progressing along a rough path of development, with stops, rests, sidepaths, and then forward movement again.

Frequency of Sessions

The overall plan and the specific frequency of the mentoring sessions are difficult issues to quantify. The usual mentoring relationship within an organizational setting, such as education, business, or government, can be conveniently scheduled as a series of three-month cycles often extended over a one-year period. The target of one to two (or more) semesters is consistent with the academic semester model. Three to six months (or longer) in the workplace can be a useful guide for a non-educational context.

Many organized mentoring programs operate with a one-year mentoring design. The relationship between the mentor and mentee is often mutually understood as concluding after about a year to allow other mentees an opportunity to be mentored, unless the program expands or is specifically designed to continue into a second year or more. The overall goals will certainly determine the pragmatic operation of the program, such as the seriousness of the efforts to recruit mentors and mentees, the allocation of administrative and clerical assistance, the resources made available to mentees (funds, trips, books, group activities and meetings), and the continued support of relevant training for mentors.

The average frequency of one-to-one meetings (using a 30–45 minute timeframe) should be one about every two weeks. Mentoring sessions could be held more often to benefit new, more high risk adult learners facing expected adjustment problems in education, or employees facing the stressful demands of personal self-assessment regarding career changes or problems related to immediate work competencies and performance. While meetings can be held less often, a concern about this overly spread-out contact is that the relationship might assume a more fragmented instead of coherent quality, losing a key element associated with the development of significant mentoring relationships.

The meetings should be scheduled for a particular time and place so that both the mentor and the mentee understand that each has made a commitment to engage in mentoring interaction on a continuing basis. The problem with unscheduled meetings or the causal "drop by when necessary" approach to mentoring is twofold. This attitude does not emphasize the importance of reasonable frequency and time spent together as relevant factors in establishing an evolving mentoring relationship nor does it usually promote the development of a truly meaningful overall experience. Mentees, of course, are always welcome to "drop by," but mentoring should be viewed as a commitment to a relatively structured but still informal style of interpersonal relationship.

To keep track of the specific content discussed in the ongoing sessions, such as the mentee's plans, goals, learning activities, concerns, and referrals, the mentor should make written but brief notes. However, these summarized entries should not be a record which emphasizes the mentee's personality, psychological, or emotional state. Instead, such notes should be maintained only for factual recall, so that the mentor is not placed in the awkward position of making such comments as: "What were we talking about last time?" The mentee could have some difficulty perceiving a mentor who claims a genuine interest in their relationship to be sincere if this same mentor has little or no idea of the mentee's specific issues from one session to another.

To capture the essence of the points raised in the mentoring sessions, the mentor could use a printed form (see Figure 9.1) as a model for recording and reviewing the content-focused aspects of the mentoring relationship. A guide to determining the type of information to record is that the mentee should be able to read these notes if this request were made, since the facts included are based on mutual mentor-mentee dialogue and often on anticipated follow-up sessions. In fact, the mentee could maintain a form similar to the

---

Mentor:_____   Mentee:_____

Session #_____   Date:_____

SUMMARY

Goals: (Personal / Academic / Training / Career)

Plans / Strategies: (Immediate / Future)

Current Learning Activities: (Informal / Formal)

Concerns: (Time / Financial / Work / Social / Family)

Referred to: (Person / Department / Office / Agency)

Figure 9.1 Mentoring session record.

one used by the mentor, and for much the same positive purpose—
to keep track of important points and information.

Matching Mentors and Mentees

Depending on the resources and goals of the organization,
the matching process can run from reasonably straightforward
to elaborate. Some programs offer prepared brochures in which

mentors list their particular interests, expertise, and philosophy of learning; this information is then used by prospective mentees as a guide to selecting mentors. In other instances, mentor-mentee pairs are assigned in advance by program administrators for a variety of reasons (field of interest, career preferences). Some programs employ tests in an attempt to match the mentor and mentee according to certain personality or cognitive-affective traits.

Obviously numerous methods can be used (Murray, 1991). But generally, a cost-effective and streamlined process should be considered as a sensible means of matching the pairs, with as much or more reliance focused on the orientations and seminars as the real source of initially stablizing the mentoring pairs and promoting their evolution into successful mentoring relationships. Whatever the specific approach to creating mentoring pairs that is most suitable for the particular group, the mentee orientation program should include a specific explanation aimed at establishing reasonable mentee expectations about the responsibilities of the mentor and the mentee.

Program administrators should introduce mentors as individuals who have made a genuine commitment of their own time, energy, and best efforts, but also indicate that mentees should not expect them to be unreal paragons of behavior. Mentees can be informed that although one of the objectives of the continuing education training seminars is to help the mentors learn to be more proficient and more adaptive to differences between themselves and their mentees, the organization cannot create the perfect match, and as mentees, they will also need to adapt to the mentors if they are to learn from the experience.

The program administrators are essentially reinforcing the message that the mentors will certainly provide the mentees with a mentoring experience based on a real attempt to fulfill the responsibilities described as the six functions of the mentor role. But in addition, they are using the earliest stage of the orientations to introduce the idea that while the mentors will try to be a significant influence in assisting mentees in their own development, mentoring is a *participatory* learning experience in which the mentees must also actively engage in order to obtain the maximum benefit. The mentee must understand that the value of the mentoring relationship will be based much less on the magical internal workings of the original mentor-mentee matching procedure and much more on the mutual ability of the pair to engage in constructive one-to-one learning.

Generally, the majority of mentees will approach mentoring as a pragmatic opportunity to advance toward their personal, educational, and career goals. A mentor and mentee should be able to develop a relatively harmonious relationship as long as the pair would have been likely to work well together if the same match had occurred as a spontaneous event. As suggested by Theriot (1986):

> Although the personality of mentors and mentees are important in mentoring relationships, the data [dissertation] showed that pairing of mentors and mentees according to their personality types is not important. . . . On the other hand, the personality of the mentor is more important than the personality of the mentee in a mentoring relationship. (p. 70)

In explaining, early in the orientation program, the particular matching process used, a primary emphasis of the program facilitator should be that the sincere efforts of both the mentor and the mentee will be required to create a meaningful learning experience.

Although the chances are generally quite favorable of a productive (perfect is not the goal) mentoring match, the right to request a "no fault" separation from a mentoring relationship, either by the mentor or the mentee, must be explained as a built-in option. However, prospective mentors and mentees must understand what the coordinators view as usual and legitimate reasons for termination of a match. Such requests should be considered as raising serious issues and could reveal early signals of unresolvable differences in the personality or approach of the mentor or mentee to one-to-one learning.

Certainly, the point is not to force a pair into a mentoring match who would *never* have voluntarily entered into or remained in it outside of the sponsored program. But if the rationale for termination is based on frivolous or unrealistic demands, or indicates a repeated pattern of problems, the coordinator may then need to confront the maturity or readiness of the mentee or mentor to currently receive or contribute to the mentoring relationship.

In addition to concerns about the match, there are other topics which have a direct bearing on the value of the mentoring experience. These important issues will be covered in the following section.

RELATED MENTORING ISSUES

In selecting specific content for presentation and discussion at the orientation and training seminars, program coordinators should introduce mentors to four anticipated influences which could impact on the quality of the mentoring experience. Of particular relevance as issues are:

1. The mentor's authority as an evaluator of the mentee's competencies

2. Gender

3. Ethnicity

4. Age

The implications of each will now be explored.

Mentors as Official Evaluators of Mentees

The evolving mentoring relationship could be compromised to some extent in the essential trust (risk of honest self-disclosure) dimension, and thus impact on other mentor role functions, if the mentor is the instructor or manager of the mentee. This is not surprising since most persons being evaluated have already learned that they should present the most positive portrait possible of themselves to those in the evaluative role. Some mentees, therefore, might view the mentoring relationship with a superior, especially if the continued employment or promotion of the mentee is directly connected to the evaluation, as primarily a self-interest opportunity to maximize their positive and minimize their negative images to those with direct and significant authority over them.

This understandable self-protective response could clearly conflict with the initial assumption of many mentors that it is in the mentees' interest as learners to acknowledge and share more private and serious concerns about their own personal abilities, competencies, and performance. Although some mentoring relationships, because of the mentees' preferences, could be centered on goal-specific issues, most mentors will not expect mentees to limit their dialogue to educational, training, and career goals.

Other possible complications are created when a mentor in a senior administrative position is actively mentoring an adult learner or employee who directly reports to and is being officially evaluated by another educator or manager lower in the same chain of command. The mentee may be unwilling to risk disclosing unfavorable perceptions about those staff at the next level above the mentee in the hierarchy of authority. Because the senior mentor will already have existing relationships with these same upper-level managers, the mentee could be uncertain about the practical impact of such revealing comments.

Mentees may be convinced that an immediate supervisor or instructor in some significant way is not providing productive assistance, or that a personally clash has occurred. But a mentee in such a situation may also decide that there are not many pragmatic options available, except to remain silent and not acknowledge that the source of a particular problem (at least to the mentee) also reports to the *same* senior mentor, but at a higher level in the organization than the mentee.

A sensible mentee would have to think that a mentor could truly be trusted before engaging in this type of personally risky disclosure. Mentees who firmly believe that the official evaluators, such as their own managers or teachers, could pose a threat if the senior mentors even unintentionally communicated the mentee's personal dissatisfaction *to them* from the subordinate's point of view, would be highly unlikely to share this type of information. In these instances, mentees could perceive the cost of honest self-disclosure as involving a potentially counterproductive and overly expensive price tag, especially if the mentees are intimidated by or do not respect the opinions or reactions of the immediate managers or educators with direct authority over them. There are a number of approaches to dealing with this problem.

First, the mentor and the mentee must initially agree that the content of the mentoring sessions is *confidential*. Neither is to reveal any of the information discussed in the sessions, especially those views which involve the personal opinions of the mentor or mentee about other persons, unless permission is requested and granted. Such violations of trust should be viewed as serious enough to be the grounds for termination of a mentoring relationship.

Of course, the major means of preventing the inappropriate and counterproductive use of information outside of the mentoring sessions which is assumed to be confidential is *not* to depend on the automatic ability of a mentee (or a mentor) to always exercise perfect judgment. In most cases, the interests and rights of all concerned would be best served if certain remarks, especially those which criticize or blame others, were discouraged within the mentoring relationship. This approach is not suggested because of the expectation that mentees or mentors would use such expressions of private thoughts and feelings for manipulative purposes.

Instead, the most likely scenario for problems would result from poor judgment. A mentee could confront an organizational superior by asserting that a senior manager (mentor), for example, disagrees with the official evaluation of the particular educator or manager regarding the mentee's competency as a report writer, and even views the individual evaluator in question as overly critical. In the act of defending the quality of the writing, the mentee might, in the heat of the moment, blurt out such a comment, which could create a triangle of tension among all three of them.

Second, the mentor should indicate an openness to exploring problems the mentee believes were *caused* by others with whom the mentee must interact. Such a discussion would be especially warranted if the mentee's personal reactions appear to be limiting learning and progress. However, the mentor cannot assume to have all of the facts, or even to be in a position to directly request or require information from those the mentee holds responsible. In reviewing the mentee's situation, the mentor should therefore emphasize that the purpose is to help the mentee within the confines of their mentoring relationship. The mentor attempts to assist the mentee, as the one facing the problem, arrive at a workable solution, not to collaborate on merely reaching consensus about the defects of others.

The mentor may need to clearly and firmly reinforce the point that attacks on the character or motives of other mentees or members of the staff are not acceptable as the legitimate content of mentoring interaction. Dialogue should be centered on the effort to understand the issues. By containing the mentee's private negative opinions about any specific individual with whom the mentee is involved, either in education or the workplace, the mentor can limit the extent to which the mentee unproductively dominates the time the mentor and mentee spend together, and thereby diminishes their positive opportunity to search for solutions. Certainly, the mentor's objective is not to suppress the mentee, but the mentor's primary interest must remain focused on the reasoned exploration of problems, solutions, and decisions, as well as on the emotional support which assists the mentee to constructively deal with issues.

The third important way of addressing the issue raised by evaluation is to remove it as a problem. Mentoring usually involves a broad developmental relationship and extends beyond a specific content emphasis, whether on academic courses or the details of on-the-job training. Mentors could reduce the mentees' concerns regarding both evaluation and confidentiality by mentoring adult learners or employees who are not in their own work-related hierarchy. A mentor who enters a mentoring relationship with any possibility of chain-of-command conflict with the mentee will need to recognize that this component might create a real trust and self-disclosure barrier in the relationship.

Moreover, both the mentor in education who uses a grade-based approach to evaluate the attainment of learning objectives, and the mentor in the workplace who uses a performance appraisal method to evaluate proficiency in work-related tasks, will need to recognize the probable impact that "for the record" evaluative feedback might have on learning when there is relatively frequent interaction between the mentor and the mentee. The interpersonal involvement which is typical of classroom instruction (faculty–adult learners) or the contact required by daily job assignments (manager–employees) generally stresses the learning of mandated and specific objectives and tasks. An underlying but unspoken theme of such a relationship could quite naturally be the highlighting of the mentee's subordinate, and therefore vulnerable, position as the learner because the emphasis on task accomplishment is often viewed as of primary importance.

Formal evaluation, though a legitimate type of assessing performance in many situations, can cause mentees to become invested in the marketing of a public image of competency to impress faculty or managerial mentors. As a result, mentees are often reinforced in their behavior to avoid self-disclosure that indicates personal anxieties or concerns about task competency. Some mentees, of course, may be comfortable with these evaluative-learning situations, remain relatively unintimidated about discussing their problems, and devote little effort to maintaining a streamlined mentee persona, but the prudent mentor probably should not anticipate such an ideal response.

Gender

The significance of gender as a factor in mentoring involves the ideas, beliefs, emotions, and specific personal experiences the mentor brings to the mentoring relationship as a male or female raised in a culture which still reinforces a variety of stereotypes regarding male versus female work-related intellectual, psychological, affective, and physical competencies. The impact of gender on the *expectations* between the mentor and mentee and on the *content* of the discussions should therefore also be considered as a potential influence (Tannen, 1990). Although an increased sensitivity to the barriers created by cultural stereotypes has been actively encouraged in the educational world as well as in the contemporary workplace, mentors may still need to address this problem if their own personal patterns of educational and career decision making, or those of the mentees, appear to have been influenced by stereotyped thinking relevant to gender.

The dynamics of the interpersonal interaction between mentor and mentee may be influenced as well by the sociocultural influence of gender (Loughlin & Mott, 1992, Williams, 1987). The present views of professionals in education, business, and government are certainly more enlightened regarding the realities of male-female educational and work-related equality, especially of females as equally competent to pursue any academic field or to function successfully in the managerial/leadership role. However, some mentors may still be unaware of the extent to which expectations of acceptable personal behavior by males and females have been molded by and still reflect unquestioned, culturally enforced perceptions.

Gender influences may affect interpersonal behavioral style. The male mentor may be oriented toward a more confrontive and less relational approach, and the female mentor may be oriented toward a less confrontive and more relational pattern of interactive behavior. These influences may be more noticeable in the male mentor-male mentee relationship, especially if the mentor expects other males to show a "tough it out" attitude (Gaylin, 1992; Witkin-Lanoil, 1986). In fact, some male mentors may have considerable difficulty accepting or responding to such behaviors as emotional discomfort, anxiety, or insecurity when verbally or nonverbally expressed in their presence by distressed male mentees because such actions are often perceived by males as character weaknesses. However, these same male mentors may be both more comfortable with and comforting to upset female mentees and view this more openly supportive behavior as the "natural" male protective reaction to what is perceived to be the more understandable, emotionally expressive behavior of "distressed females."

By contrast, the female mentor may have been socialized to behave in a more nurturing and relationally orientated manner with both males and females, and therefore be more generally comfortable with expressing supportive rather than confrontive behaviors (Gilligan, 1982; Witkin-Lanoil, 1984). While male and female mentees certainly could benefit from the often sensitive and supportive mentoring experience offered by many female mentors, they might not receive the necessary confrontive feedback required of a balanced mentoring relationship, which female mentors might have more of a tendency to avoid.

Moreover, some male mentees might be concerned that they were not receiving enough of the legitimate feedback and advice they had expected, even from a female mentor who they anticipated would be gentler about critiques than a male. By contrast, female mentees might react negatively to tough comments from a female mentor, though they might tolerate the same views from a male mentor, because they expected the female to be more nurturing and less confrontive. Female mentees might also be reluctant to openly challenge a male mentor who in fact is dominating their mentoring relationship.

Another concern regarding gender is the real problem of the perceived romantic or undue influence implications of an older male mentor independently encouraging a mentoring relationship with a younger female. Such an initiative, though completely free of any motive other than to professionally mentor another person, could be misinterpreted by the mentee as well as by other members of the staff (Jeruchim & Shapiro, 1992). Also, female mentors whose intent is to initiate only professional mentoring relationships with male mentees could be subject to the same unfortunate pressures. This aspect of the gender issue explains the reluctance of some mentors to personally—when separated from the official sanction of a planned mentoring program—establish mentoring relationships with their students or employees. Institutionally sponsored programs clearly help defuse the problems associated with this particular issue.

Ethnicity

The influence of ethnicity differences between the mentor and the mentee should also be reviewed (McGoldrick, Pearce, & Giordano, 1982). Prejudice toward others of different racial, religious, and ethnic backgrounds is not likely to be overtly expressed by mentors or mentees within more diversity-conscious modern educational and employment environments. Instead, these differences may manifest as stereotyped perceptions of others without the conscious realization that such a powerful negative influence has entered into the mentoring relationship. The consequences of these more subtle attitudes or beliefs about persons of different ethnic origins or socioeconomic backgrounds may include such problems as the mentor's prior expectation of the mentee's proper educational major or the mentor's distorted view of the mentee's probable effectiveness in a particular work-related task or situation.

Mentors will also need to be aware of the unacknowledged stereotyping emanating from mentees' own backgrounds and be prepared to carefully raise concerns about false assumptions and unsubstantiated views. Such dialogues, during which mentors appropriately challenge prejudiced views, can significantly contribute to mentees' personal and sociocultural growth. In addition, the mentor will need to be especially alert and sensitive to legitimate mutual differences in ideas and beliefs, as well as verbal and nonverbal behaviors. These could inadvertently cause potential misunderstanding or misinterpretation if not openly addressed and approached as mutual learning within the mentor-mentee relationship. The principle of respecting differences is a foundation stone of mentoring.

Age

The age of the mentor can be an influence on the mentoring relationship. In the traditional model of mentoring, the mentor has usually been older, more educated, more experienced, and more professionally accomplished than the mentee. These expected differences appear consistent with the historical role of the wise mentor. Since the current population of adult learners and employees indicates that the age ranges of mentees may vary from 18 to 50+, mentors may be entering into relationships with mentees older than themselves or at least much closer in age (Schlossberg, Lynch, & Chickering, 1989).

While mentor age may not always dramatically impact on the interpersonal dynamics of mentoring, there are some genuine concerns relevant to differences in age between the mentor and the mentee. If the mentor is almost 20 years older or more, and if the mentee is in the early twenties, the mentoring relationship may assume some of the characteristics of parent-child interaction. This could introduce other unresolved conflicts, especially if self-identity and dependency are still major issues for the mentee. If the mentor is closer in age to the mentee, the relationship may reflect some of the characteristics of peer interaction, and thereby reduce the mentee's perception of the mentor as a wiser, more experienced educator/manager role model.

Because the mentor is neither parent nor peer, the astute mentor will need to be alert to the importance of maintaining the mentor role if the age factor appears to be creating an interpersonal relationship problem for the mentee which could reduce the mentor's effectiveness. The mentor may need to openly address skeptical mentee responses which appear related to issues of mentor age. Older mentees will likely face other mentoring experiences with younger mentors in education or the workplace. Instead of treating the current situation as a rare occurrence, the mentor should approach it as an opportunity for the mentee to adapt—to learn that helpful mentors, now and in future, may vary considerably in age.

Also, the mentor will of necessity be at a level of attainment which involves being more of the technical expert—more well-trained and educated, as well as more experienced (usually) in the personal and social skills required for goal achievement in the field. If this is not the case, then what would be the rationale for the mentoring relationship? However, mentors younger than their mentees should recognize the possible difficulties created by interaction with mentees with more quantitative life experience, especially those who quickly assume that their mentors can offer only limited assistance with experience-based problems. Often, though certainly not always, the younger mentor may have valuable advice and should not hesitate to offer it.

Attention and energies should be focused on the six functions of the complete mentor role, as well as the expected developmental phases of the mentoring relationship. While age sometimes complicates the interpersonal dynamics of mentoring, it does not present an insurmountable block.

MENTORING CONTEXT

Organizational variations which influence the mentoring context can account for differences in the perception of mentor-mentee goals. In education, professionals who serve as mentors are viewed as in harmony with the general philosophy of promoting personal, educational, and career development. Mentors of adult learners in postsecondary education are therefore usually regarded as *already* cast in the role of educator (Schlossberg, Lynch, & Chickering, 1989). However, the role of the mentor in government and business has not been generally viewed in an identical way (Kram, 1985).

The premise driving traditional business manager-employee interactions, when re-labeled as mentor-mentee relationships, often is that the mentoring model relevant to education is not directly transferrable over to the profit-equals-survival demands of a business or to the public service and accountability agenda of employees in government. The objectives of business and government organizations—profit or service—are referenced as the critical reason why the mentoring relationship and certain mentor behaviors are different than the model appropriate for an educational institution.

This conceptual distinction has led to organizational differences in the approach to mentoring goals and behavioral process. It accounts for the general perception by mentors in business that the general development of the mentee as a *learner* is not really the primary task—and that the business mentoring relationship is essentially the means to an end more closely identified with larger organizational performance issues. The contribution to the specific and immediate competitiveness and productivity of the organization, not surprisingly, is therefore initially perceived as the overriding *utilitarian* purpose of mentoring. The generic developmental potential of promoting adult learning is a secondary and even separate concern.

This often means that overall value to the goals of the institution takes precedence over specific benefits to the individual. Such a powerful belief can block managers in the daily world of one-to-one interpersonal interaction with employees from completing a behavioral transition into the contemporary mentor role of adult educator. In this functionally orientiated approach to adult learning, employee development is often applied, via training programs, as more of a productivity concept, with personnel viewed as individuals who primarily need to be well-trained to perform their jobs (Sayles, 1993).

Human relations training and initiatives have shown definite and sometimes dramatic results in recent years. But as experienced observers have noted, the shift to behaviorally encouraged and rewarded, independent worker behavior, and away from the more dependent employee culture of the past, has been slow in manifesting as the overall daily reality of organizational life (Belasco, 1991; Covey, 1989). Although this point is not intended to suggest an improper or simplistic training mentality mindset of those responsible for human resource management, the objective of promoting holistic adult learning is often not a significant goal of the education/training component of employees' professional development. In the mentoring relationships which occur outside traditional educational environments, such as business and government, more of an emphasis will need to be placed on the teaching function of the mentors (managers) viewed as adult educators, and the learning function of mentees (employees) viewed as adult learners.

The education context also has some unique problems. The philosophical assumption by educators that the cognitive, affective, and career development of the mentee as an adult learner was the primary purpose of mentoring generally did provide a productive operational guide to the creation of mentoring programs. In the world of education, however, the same powerful and dominant idea that mentoring relationships were primarily initiated for the benefit of adult learners often coexisted with the perception that the professional staff involved as mentors would naturally transfer over to mentoring interactions their *already* developed behavioral proficiencies from previous involvement with students (Schlossberg, Lynch, & Chickering, 1989). Sometimes, this unquestioned perception promoted a naive belief in the power of the existing mentoring context—education—to intrinsically create successful mentor-mentee relationships.

The prevalent view that the prior training and experience of educators would *predetermine* the success of newly created, organizationally sponsored mentoring programs within education was often so entrenched that the almost exclusive concern of program sponsors was to locate mentor volunteers and match them with mentees. After that, the development of meaningful interaction between mentors and mentees was assumed to inherently germinate in the fertile soil of education. This expectation, of course, often proved to be based on a highly oversimplified view of context itself as capable of conferring competence, without specific mentor training, mentee orientation, or proper attention to the administration of the mentor program.

In terms of general preparation, mentors within education should not necessarily be considered as already more behaviorally adept than those in business, nor assumed to need little or no training in the mentor role. Mentors inside education, however, may often believe themselves to be immediately capable of demonstrating the mentoring behaviors required to establish a successful mentor-mentee relationship because it occurs in the context of the familiar learning environment of postsecondary education. Therefore, they may not initially consider the importance of examining the distinction between their role as faculty or administrators and their actual behavioral competency in the mentor role.

SUMMARY

Contemporary mentoring relationships are considered to be one-to-one learning experiences that are directly influenced by mentor competency in six interrelated behavioral functions. Mentors fulfill the complete mentor role by serving as a consistent source of emotional support (even when confrontive), practical information and advice, challenge and inspiration, and experiential wisdom, all of which are offered to fulfill and expand the personal, educational, and career objectives and opportunities of mentees.

Planners of mentoring programs are urged to develop an overall strategic plan of carefully conducted recruitment campaigns, orientations, and seminars which are designed to promote, enhance, and sustain the mentoring model of learning. Issues which impact on mentor-mentee interaction, such as administrative resources, the mentoring match, frequency and length of sessions, mentoring goals and context, mentee expectations, authority of mentor, ethnicity, gender, and age are presented as important topics for review.

The personal and professional background of those who volunteer to mentor is viewed as a rich reservoir that is offered to help mentees maximize their individual potential. But mentors who have already achieved success in their own lives and careers are also described as benefiting from reflection on their individual competency in the mentor role through self-initiated assessments as well as from critiques offered by appropriate others. As adult learners themselves, mentors particularly value pragmatic guidance which enables them to realistically fuse their good intentions with truly helpful mentoring behaviors so that they can more effectively assist and enrich mentees on their own unique journeys of discovery. A continuing education approach is advocated to help mentors increase their understanding of the mentor role and to strengthen the constructive interpersonal dialogue of the evolving mentor-mentee relationship. Scheduled hands-on training, such as that offered by role simulation, observation, and feedback, is of particular relevance in developing the interpersonal skills mentors need to properly influence mentees. When conducted in a psychological climate of nonthreatening but direct comments, small group seminars especially offer inexperienced mentors the advantage of personal participation as they practice under supervision to become more proficient at applying their knowledge.

In our society, much attention is directed at the responsibility of adults as *learners* in education, business, and government. And such a legitimate expectation is not misplaced. This work, however, emphasizes the primary importance of mentors as informed and proactive practitioners in creating successful mentoring interactions *with* adult learners. The mentor, in undertaking the ambitious goals of mentoring, participates as a meaningful, if often transitory, figure in the life of a mentee without being parent or peer. Mentors are not distant and idealized role models, but rather approachable, reasonable, and competent individuals with ideals who are actively committed to positive contributions on behalf of a diverse population of adult learners.

APPENDIXES

APPENDIX A

Principles of Adult Mentoring Scale — Postsecondary Education (PSE)

Includes:

***INSTRUCTIONS FOR SCORING AND
  INTERPRETING: POSTSECONDARY EDUCATION**

*SCORING SHEET: POSTSECONDARY EDUCATION

***MENTOR ROLE COMPETENCIES:
  POSTSECONDARY EDUCATION**

Principles of Adult Mentoring Scale— Postsecondary Education

INSTRUCTIONS FOR COMPLETING:

Circle *one* of the following choices for each of the 55 statements that is *most representative of your actual behavior as a mentor:*

Never   Infrequently   Sometimes   Frequently   Always

Note:

- If you have functioned as a mentor, your answers should be based on your *past* (and if applicable, *current*) mentoring experience.
- If you have very little or no actual experience as a mentor of adults, your answers should be based on how you would *probably* interact at this time with a mentee.

Answer *all* of the statements. Then refer to the *Instructions for Scoring and Interpreting* which is located at the end of the scale.

SCALE STATEMENTS

1. I encourage students to express their honest feelings (positive and negative) about their academic and social experiences as adult learners in college.

Never   Infrequently   Sometimes   Frequently   Always

2. I discuss with students who are discouraged (due to poor scholastic performance or other difficulties) the importance of developing a realistic view of learning that can include both success and disappointment (mentioning other students who have been frustrated as learners but have continued their education).

Never   Infrequently   Sometimes   Frequently   Always

3. I ask students for detailed information about their academic progress.

Never   Infrequently   Sometimes   Frequently   Always

4. I refer students to other staff members and departments to obtain information they need about academic and career plans.

Never   Infrequently   Sometimes   Frequently   Always

5. I attempt to be verbally supportive when students are emotionally upset.

Never   Infrequently   Sometimes   Frequently   Always

6. I suggest to students that we establish a regular schedule of meeting times.

Never   Infrequently   Sometimes   Frequently   Always

7. I make a good deal of eye contact with students.

Never   Infrequently   Sometimes   Frequently   Always

8. I suggest that students who indicate concerns about serious emotional or psychological problems meet with a college counselor.

Never   Infrequently   Sometimes   Frequently   Always

9. I ask students to explain (in some detail) the reasons for their college plans and career choices.

Never   Infrequently   Sometimes   Frequently   Always

10. I encourage students to provide a good deal of background information about their academic preparation, success, and problems in college.

Never   Infrequently   Sometimes   Frequently   Always

11. I inquire in some depth about students' study strategies and (if necessary) offer practical suggestions and/or refer them for help to improve their academic performance.

Never   Infrequently   Sometimes   Frequently   Always

12. I explain to students that I really want to know what they as

individuals honestly think about issues (such as balancing college commitments and outside responsibilities) so that I can offer advice specific to them.

Never   Infrequently   Sometimes   Frequently   Always

13. I arrange my meetings (when possible) with students at times when I will probably not be interrupted very much by telephone calls or other people.

Never   Infrequently   Sometimes   Frequently   Always

14. I explain the need to explore degree and career options to students who have insufficient information (such as adult learners in transition between job fields or facing long-term commitments to fulfill degree requirements).

Never   Infrequently   Sometimes   Frequently   Always

15. I encourage students to consider nontraditional (such as television-based) courses as well as more formal educational opportunities they have not yet explored to develop their personal interests.

Never   Infrequently   Sometimes   Frequently   Always

16. I point out inconsistencies (rationalizations) in students' explanations of why their academic goals were not achieved if I believe my comments will help them develop better coping strategies to deal with their problem.

Never   Infrequently   Sometimes   Frequently   Always

17. I try to stimulate students to do more rigorous critical thinking about the long-range implications (time commitments, lifestyle changes) their academic choices may have for increasing the complexity of their lives.

Never   Infrequently   Sometimes   Frequently   Always

18. I explain to students why they should discuss (even with someone else) significant academic problems they are presently confronted with even if they prefer not to deal with these issues.

Never   Infrequently   Sometimes   Frequently   Always

19. I offer recommendations to students about their personal academic learning needs (from remedial to honors courses, tutoring, course loads) based on specific information provided by them (as well as placement tests and academic records, if available) during our meetings.

Never   Infrequently   Sometimes   Frequently   Always

20. I follow up on students' decisions to develop better personal strategies (study habits, getting accurate information, making realistic decisions) by asking questions (and offering comments, if appropriate) about their actual progress at later meetings.

Never   Infrequently   Sometimes   Frequently   Always

21. I tell students when I think their ideas about career or academic concerns (such as job entry or degree requirements) are very clearly based on incomplete or inaccurate information.

Never   Infrequently   Sometimes   Frequently   Always

22. I attempt to guide students in exploring their own personal commitment to career or academic interests by posing alternative views for them to consider.

Never   Infrequently   Sometimes   Frequently   Always

23. I verbally communicate my concerns to students when their negative attitudes and emotions are expressed to me through such nonverbal behaviors as eye contact, facial expression, and voice tone.

Never   Infrequently   Sometimes   Frequently   Always

24. I discuss students' general reasons for attending college and then focus on helping them identify concrete educational objectives, degrees, curricula, and courses.

Never   Infrequently   Sometimes   Frequently   Always

25. I provide a reasonable amount of guidance in our discussions so that students will explore realistic options and attainable academic and career objectives.

Never   Infrequently   Sometimes   Frequently   Always

26. I ask students to review their strategies for managing the changes in their lives (such as impact of increased time pressures on personal relationships or ability to handle current job) while they pursue their "dreams" regarding educational goals.

Never   Infrequently   Sometimes   Frequently   Always

27. I question students' assumptions (especially about career options and the value of education) as a way of guiding them through a realistic appraisal of the extent to which their important ideas and beliefs are based on adequate personal experiences and facts.

Never   Infrequently   Sometimes   Frequently   Always

28. I discuss my own work-related experience as a way of helping students think about and carefully examine their career options.

Never   Infrequently   Sometimes   Frequently   Always

29. I share with students personal examples of difficulties I have overcome in my own individual and professional growth if these experiences might provide insights for them.

Never   Infrequently   Sometimes   Frequently   Always

30. I engage students in discussions which require them to reflect on the new competencies they will need to achieve their future goals.

Never   Infrequently   Sometimes   Frequently   Always

31. I point out (using personal examples as well as stories about students) that achievement in college is primarily based on personal commitment (rather than just "luck") to students who are having problems completing the work but appear unrealistic about the amount of discipline and energy needed to cope with the pressures of an academic workload.

Never   Infrequently   Sometimes   Frequently   Always

32. I express my personal confidence in the ability of students to succeed if they persevere in the pursuit of their academic goals.

Never   Infrequently   Sometimes   Frequently   Always

33. I confront students with the reality of continued or probable

negative consequences in a direct (but supportive) manner when they repeatedly do not follow through on their stated intentions to deal with serious academic problems.

Never   Infrequently   Sometimes   Frequently   Always

34. I encourage students to use me as a sounding board to explore their hopes, ideas, feelings, and plans.

Never   Infrequently   Sometimes   Frequently   Always

35. I engage students in discussions aimed at motivating them to develop a positive view of their ability to function now and in the future as independent, competent adult learners.

Never   Infrequently   Sometimes   Frequently   Always

36. I use my own experience (personal as well as references to other students I have advised) to explain how college courses or activities students believe will be boring, too demanding, or not relevant could be valuable learning experiences for them.

Never   Infrequently   Sometimes   Frequently   Always

37. I offer students constructive criticism if I believe their avoidance of problems and decisions is clearly limiting their growth as adult learners.

Never   Infrequently   Sometimes   Frequently   Always

38. I encourage students to make well-informed personal choices as they plan their own educational and career goals.

Never   Infrequently   Sometimes   Frequently   Always

39. I explore with students who express a lack of confidence in themselves the ways in which their own life experience might be a valuable resource to help them devise strategies to succeed within the college environment.

Never   Infrequently   Sometimes   Frequently   Always

40. I assist students in using facts to carefully map out realistic, step-by-step strategies to achieve their academic and career goals.

Never   Infrequently   Sometimes   Frequently   Always

41. I share my own views and feelings when they are relevant to the college-related situations and issues I am discussing with students.

Never   Infrequently   Sometimes   Frequently   Always

42. I listen to criticism from students about college policies, regulations, requirements, and even colleagues without immediately attempting to offer justifications.

Never   Infrequently   Sometimes   Frequently   Always

43. I offer comments to students about their inappropriate behavior (in college) if I have a reasonable expectation that they are prepared to work on positive change and will most likely experience some success as a result.

Never   Infrequently   Sometimes   Frequently   Always

44. I inform students that they can discuss "negative" emotions such as anxiety, self-doubt, fear, and anger in our meetings.

Never   Infrequently   Sometimes   Frequently   Always

45. I express confidence in students' abilities to achieve their educational goat, especially when they are having personal difficulties in fulfilling their academic responsibilities due to outside pressures (work, family, relationships).

Never   Infrequently   Sometimes   Frequently   Always

46. I question students' decisions and actions regarding college-related issues and problems when they do not appear to be appropriate solutions.

Never   Infrequently   Sometimes   Frequently   Always

47. I discuss the positive and negative feelings students have about their abilities to succeed as adult learners.

Never   Infrequently   Sometimes   Frequently   Always

48. I offer as few carefully chosen criticisms as possible when I try to get students to understand the (often difficult to accept) con-

nection between their own self-limiting (defeating) behaviors and their inability to solve a particular problem.

Never   Infrequently   Sometimes   Frequently   Always

49. I ask probing questions that require more than a "yes" or "no" answer so that students will explain (in some detail) their views regarding their academic progress and plans.

Never   Infrequently   Sometimes   Frequently   Always

50. I explore with students the extent of their commitment (such as willingness to spend time and energy) as adult learners in achieving their educational goals.

Never   Infrequently   Sometimes   Frequently   Always

51. I base the timing of my "confrontive" questions and comments to students on my knowledge of their individual readiness (often related to the stage of our relationship) to benefit from discussions about clearly sensitive issues.

Never   Infrequently   Sometimes   Frequently   Always

52. I discuss my role as a mentor with students so that their individual expectations of me are appropriate and realistic.

Never   Infrequently   Sometimes   Frequently   Always

53. I try to clarify the problems students are explaining to me by verbally expressing my understanding of their feelings and then asking if my views are accurate.

Never   Infrequently   Sometimes   Frequently   Always

54. I ask students to reflect on the resources available (college, family, community) to help them manage their lives effectively while they pursue their educational and career goals.

Never   Infrequently   Sometimes   Frequently   Always

55. I emphasize to students, especially those who appear uncertain about what to expect from our meetings, that one of my im-

portant goals is to assist them in reaching their own decisions about personal, academic, and career goals.

Never   Infrequently   Sometimes   Frequently   Always

INSTRUCTIONS FOR SCORING AND INTERPRETING: POSTSECONDARY EDUCATION

1. The point value for each answer is listed below:

Never	1 point
Infrequently	2 points
Sometimes	3 points
Frequently	4 points
Always	5 points

2. Refer to the *Scoring Sheet: Postsecondary Education* for the item statements of the scale (*Items* are identified with numbers) which are specifically listed under each of the six factors: Relationship Emphasis, Information Emphasis, Facilitative Focus, Confrontive Focus, Mentor Model, and Student Vision.

3. Enter the point value (1 to 5 points) on the *Points* line which is below each of the numbered *Items*. For example, using "Factor 1: Relationship Emphasis," if you had circled as the answer to item statement "1" the word "Sometimes," then a "3" (points value) would be entered directly below the "1" on the *Scoring Sheet*. Then you would total all of the points recorded for "Factor 1" and enter the cumulative score on the (*total*) line.

4. After determining the total for each of the six separate factor item scores, then total *all* of the six separate factor scores and enter this overall score at the bottom of the sheet on the *Grand Total for Overall Score* line.

5. Refer to the *Mentor Role Competencies: Postsecondary Education* chart. Enter the *Grand Total for Overall Score* in the appro-

priate block under *Overall Score*. Then enter the separate (*total*) score for each of the six factors in the appropriate block for the specific factor: Relationship Emphasis, Information Emphasis, Facilitative Focus, Confrontive Focus, Mentor Model, and Student Vision.

6. Interpret scores in the ranges labeled *not effective* and *less effective* as indicating a need for professional improvement. A score in the *effective* category indicates a general competency with opportunity for improvement. Interpret *very effective* and *highly effective* as indicating positive mentoring behavioral skills (which could still be fine tuned).

7. Refer to Appendix C: The Mentor Role: Six Behavioral Functions for the definition, purpose, and mentor behaviors associated with each of the six separate mentor functions. Consider all six of the mentor functions as a description of the complete (integrated) mentor role.

SCORING SHEET: POSTSECONDARY EDUCATION

Factor 1: Relationship Emphasis

Items: 1, 5, 7, 12, 13, 23, 42, 44, 47, 53   Relationship

Points: __ __ __ __ __ __ __ __ __ __
_____
(total)

Factor 2: Information Emphasis

Items: 3, 4, 6, 9, 10, 11, 19, 24, 40, 52   Information

Points: __ __ __ __ __ __ __ __ __ __
_____
(total)

Factor 3: Facilitative Focus

Items: 15, 22, 25, 34, 39, 49   Facilitative

Points: __ __ __ __ __ __
_____
(total)

Factor 4: Confrontive Focus

Items: 8, 16, 18, 21, 27, 31, 33, 37, 43, 46, 48, 51 Confrontive

Points: __ __ __ __ __ __ __ __ __ __ __ __
_____
(total)

Factor 5: Mentor Model

Items: 2, 28, 29, 32, 36, 41   Mentor

Points: __ __ __ __ __ __
_____
(total)

Factor 6: Student Vision

Items: 14, 17, 20, 26, 30, 35, 38, 45, 50, 54, 55   Student

Points: __ __ __ __ __ __ __ __ __ __ __
_____
(total)

Grand Total for Overall Score: _____

MENTOR ROLE COMPETENCIES:
POSTSECONDARY EDUCATION

Overall Score

55–190	191–205	206–219	220–234	235–275
not effective	less effective	effective	very effective	highly effective

Relationship Emphasis

10–35	36–38	39–41	42–44	45–50
not effective	less effective	effective	very effective	highly effective

Information Emphasis

10–33	34–36	37–39	40–42	43–50
not effective	less effective	effective	very effective	highly effective

Facilitative Focus

6–18	19–20	21–22	23–24	25–30
not effective	less effective	effective	very effective	highly effective

Confrontive Focus

12–39	40–43	44–46	47–50	51–60
not effective	less effective	effective	very effective	highly effective

Mentor Model

6–18	19–21	22–23	24–25	26–30
not effective	less effective	effective	very effective	highly effective

Student Vision

11–37	38–41	42–44	45–47	48–55
not effective	less effective	effective	very effective	highly effective

APPENDIX B

Principles of Adult Mentoring Scale—
Business and Government (B&G)

Includes:

***INSTRUCTIONS FOR SCORING AND
INTERPRETING: BUSINESS AND GOVERNMENT**

*SCORING SHEET: BUSINESS AND GOVERNMENT

***MENTOR ROLE COMPETENCIES:
BUSINESS AND GOVERNMENT**

Principles of Adult Mentoring Scale—Business and Government

INSTRUCTIONS FOR COMPLETING:

Circle *one* of the following choices for each of the 55 statements that is *most representative of your actual behavior as a mentor.*

Never   Infrequently   Sometimes   Frequently   Always

Note:

- If you have functioned as a mentor, your answers should be based on your *past* (and if, applicable, *current*) mentoring experience.
- If you have very little or no actual experience as a mentor of adults, your answers should be based on how you would *probably* interact at this time with a mentee.

Answer *all* of the statements. Then refer to the *Instructions for Scoring and Interpreting* which is located at the end of the scale.

SCALE STATEMENTS

1. I encourage employees to express their honest feelings (positive or negative) about their work-related experiences (including such dimensions as training, educational opportunities, and social relationships).

Never   Infrequently   Sometimes   Frequently   Always

2. I discuss with employees who are discouraged (due to lack of promotion or other difficulties) the importance of developing a realistic view of work-related advancement that can include both success and disappointment (mentioning, for example, other employees who have been frustrated but still continued to explore opportu-

nities to learn and enhance their marketable knowledge, skills, and behaviors at work).

Never   Infrequently   Sometimes   Frequently   Always

3. I ask employees for detailed information about their progress in learning all aspects of their job.

Never   Infrequently   Sometimes   Frequently   Always

4. I refer employees to other staff members and departments to obtain information relevant to pursuing their individual educational, training, and career development plans.

Never   Infrequently   Sometimes   Frequently   Always

5. I attempt to be verbally supportive when employees are emotionally upset.

Never   Infrequently   Sometimes   Frequently   Always

6. I suggest to employees that we establish a regular schedule of meeting times.

Never   Infrequently   Sometimes   Frequently   Always

7. I make a good deal of eye contact with employees during our meetings.

Never   Infrequently   Sometimes   Frequently   Always

8. I suggest that employees who indicate concerns about serious emotional or psychological problems meet with a counselor (if they have not already done so) responsible for assisting employees in the workplace (or suggest they consult with a professional outside the workplace, if necessary).

Never   Infrequently   Sometimes   Frequently   Always

9. I ask employees to identify their career choices and to explain their strategies for continuing work-related training and learning to support the achievement of these career goals.

Never   Infrequently   Sometimes   Frequently   Always

10. I encourage employees to provide a good deal of background information about their preparation, success, and problems in pursuing their career plans.

Never Infrequently Sometimes Frequently Always

11. I inquire in some depth about employees' strategies for utilizing workplace resources to increase their on-the-job learning and (if necessary) offer practical suggestions and/or refer them for assistance to improve their job performance.

Never Infrequently Sometimes Frequently Always

12. I explain to employees that I really want to know what they as individuals honestly think about issues (such as balancing job requirements and/or career development commitments and outside responsibilities) so that I can offer advice specific to them.

Never Infrequently Sometimes Frequently Always

13. I arrange my meetings (when possible) with employees at times when I will probably not be interrupted very much by telephone calls or other people.

Never Infrequently Sometimes Frequently Always

14. I point out to employees the necessity of obtaining accurate and detailed information about their career options, especially those who have insufficient factual information about such issues as additional and/or changing work-related training and educational requirements or preparing for the personal psychological/emotional transition between job fields.

Never Infrequently Sometimes Frequently Always

15. I encourage employees to consider "nontraditional" (such as television and correspondence-based) courses as well as more formal educational opportunities to develop their career interests.

Never Infrequently Sometimes Frequently Always

16. I point out inconsistencies (rationalizations) in employees' explanations of why their job performance and/or career goals were

not achieved if I believe my comments will help them develop better coping strategies to deal with their problems.

Never   Infrequently   Sometimes   Frequently   Always

17. I try to stimulate employees to do more rigorous critical thinking about the long-range implications (time and energy commitments for additional training and education) their career choices may have for increasing the complexity of their lives to help them plan, prepare, and adapt to "predictable" lifestyle changes.

Never   Infrequently   Sometimes   Frequently   Always

18. I explain to employees why they should discuss (even with someone else) significant work-related problems they are presently confronted with even if they prefer not to deal with these issues.

Never   Infrequently   Sometimes   Frequently   Always

19. I offer recommendations to employees about their current and future training and educational needs (from basic to advanced skills and learning) based on specific information provided by them regarding their history of previous training, experience, and academic/technical preparation.

Never   Infrequently   Sometimes   Frequently   Always

20. I follow up on employees' stated goals to develop better personal decision-making strategies relevant to career and educational planning (such as obtaining current information and researching multiple sources) by asking questions and/or offering comments about their actual progress at later meetings.

Never   Infrequently   Sometimes   Frequently   Always

21. I tell employees when I think their ideas about career or educational concerns (such as promotional opportunity, entry into a different job, or future training and degree requirements) are very clearly based on incomplete or inaccurate information.

Never   Infrequently   Sometimes   Frequently   Always

22. I attempt to guide employees in exploring their own personal commitment to their stated career and work-related educational in-

terests by posing alternative views (such as other career and training/education options) for them to consider.

Never   Infrequently   Sometimes   Frequently   Always

23. I verbally communicate my concerns to employees when their negative attitudes and emotions are expressed to me through such nonverbal behaviors as eye contact, facial expression, and voice tone.

Never   Infrequently   Sometimes   Frequently   Always

24. I discuss employees' general reasons for planning to obtain additional work-related educational credentials or training and then focus on helping them identify concrete degrees, curricula, courses, and workshops.

Never   Infrequently   Sometimes   Frequently   Always

25. I provide a reasonable amount of factual guidance in our discussions so that employees will explore realistic options and attainable career objectives.

Never   Infrequently   Sometimes   Frequently   Always

26. I ask employees to review their plans for managing the current or anticipated changes in their personal lives (such as impact of increased pressures on their family and social relationships) while they pursue their job and career-related educational goals.

Never   Infrequently   Sometimes   Frequently   Always

27. I question employees' assumptions (especially about career options and the choice of additional training and education) as a way of guiding them through a realistic appraisal of the extent to which their important ideas and beliefs are based on adequate personal experiences and facts.

Never   Infrequently   Sometimes   Frequently   Always

28. I discuss my own work-related experience as a way of helping employees think about and carefully examine their career options.

Never   Infrequently   Sometimes   Frequently   Always

29. I share with employees personal examples of difficulties I have overcome in my own individual and professional growth if these experiences might provide insights for them.

Never   Infrequently   Sometimes   Frequently   Always

30. I engage employees in discussions which require them to reflect on the new competencies they will need to achieve their future goals.

Never   Infrequently   Sometimes   Frequently   Always

31. I point out (using personal examples as well as stories about other employees) that career achievement is primarily based on personal commitment and planning (rather than just "luck") to employees who are having problems completing all of their job and educational (training and/or academic course assignments) but appear unrealistic about the amount of discipline and energy needed to cope with the pressures of contemporary career advancement.

Never   Infrequently   Sometimes   Frequently   Always

32. I express my personal confidence in the ability of employees to succeed if they persevere in the pursuit of their career goals.

Never   Infrequently   Sometimes   Frequently   Always

33. I confront employees with the reality of continued or probable negative consequences in a direct (but supportive) manner when they repeatedly do not follow through on their stated intentions to deal with serious job and/or career-related problems.

Never   Infrequently   Sometimes   Frequently   Always

34. I encourage employees to use me as a sounding board to explore their work-related hopes, ideas, feelings, and plans.

Never   Infrequently   Sometimes   Frequently   Always

35. I engage employees in discussions aimed at motivating them to develop a positive view of their ability to function now and in the future as independent, competent adult learners in the workplace environment.

Never   Infrequently   Sometimes   Frequently   Always

36. I use my own experience (personal as well as references to other employees I have advised) to explain how training workshops, educational programs, and job rotational opportunities that employees believe will not be career-relevant could in fact be valuable work-related learning experiences for them.

Never   Infrequently   Sometimes   Frequently   Always

37. I offer employees constructive criticism if I believe their avoidance of problems and decisions is clearly limiting their work performance and/or career potential.

Never   Infrequently   Sometimes   Frequently   Always

38. I encourage employees to make well-informed and critically reflective personal choices as they plan their career experience, training, and educational goals.

Never   Infrequently   Sometimes   Frequently   Always

39. I explore with employees who express a lack of confidence in themselves the ways in which their own life experiences might be a valuable resource to help them devise strategies to succeed within the workplace environment.

Never   Infrequently   Sometimes   Frequently   Always

40. I assist employees in using facts to carefully map out realistic step-by-step strategies to achieve their career, training, and educational goals.

Never   Infrequently   Sometimes   Frequently   Always

41. I share my views and feelings when they are relevant to the work-related situations and issues I am discussing with employees.

Never   Infrequently   Sometimes   Frequently   Always

42. I listen to criticism from employees about work-related policies, regulations, requirements, and even colleagues without immediately attempting to offer justifications.

Never   Infrequently   Sometimes   Frequently   Always

43. I offer comments to employees about what appears to be their

own inappropriate or ineffective behavior at work (based on their own explanations and descriptions) if I have a reasonable expectation that they are prepared to work on positive change and will most likely experience some success as a result.

Never   Infrequently   Sometimes   Frequently   Always

44. I inform employees that they can discuss their "negative" emotions relevant to the workplace (such as anxiety, self-doubt, fear, and anger) in our meetings.

Never   Infrequently   Sometimes   Frequently   Always

45. I express confidence in employees' abilities to achieve their career-related educational and training goals, especially when they are having personal difficulties in fulfilling their educational responsibilities due to pressures from work, family, or social relationships.

Never   Infrequently   Sometimes   Frequently   Always

46. I question employees' decisions and actions regarding past and current work-related issues and problems when they do not appear to have formulated and/or implemented appropriate solutions.

Never   Infrequently   Sometimes   Frequently   Always

47. I discuss the positive and negative feelings employees have about their abilities to succeed in their careers.

Never   Infrequently   Sometimes   Frequently   Always

48. I offer as few carefully chosen criticisms as possible when I try to get employees to understand the (often difficult to accept) connection between their own self-limiting (defeating) behaviors and their inability to solve a particular work-related problem.

Never   Infrequently   Sometimes   Frequently   Always

49. I ask probing questions that require more than a "yes" or "no" answer so that employees will explain (in some detail) their views regarding their career plans and progress.

Never   Infrequently   Sometimes   Frequently   Always

50. I explore with employees the extent of their commitment (such as willingness to spend time and energy as continuing adult learners in training, education, and job-related learning such as TQM) in achieving their career goals.

Never   Infrequently   Sometimes   Frequently   Always

51. I base the timing of my "confrontive" questions and comments to employees on my knowledge of their individual readiness (often related to the stage of our relationship) to benefit from discussions about clearly sensitive work-related issues.

Never   Infrequently   Sometimes   Frequently   Always

52. I discuss my role as a mentor with employees so that their individual expectations of me are appropriate and realistic.

Never   Infrequently   Sometimes   Frequently   Always

53. I try to clarify the problems employees are explaining to me by verbally expressing my understanding of their feelings and then asking if my views are accurate.

Never   Infrequently   Sometimes   Frequently   Always

54. I ask employees to reflect on and explore the resources available (government-sponsored training and assistance, college courses and programs, community-based organizations and workshops, family and social relationships) to help them manage the change and stress in their lives more effectively while they pursue their career and educational goals.

Never   Infrequently   Sometimes   Frequently   Always

55. I emphasize to employees, especially those who appear uncertain about what to expect from our meetings, that one of my important objectives as a mentor is to be of assistance to them in their personal progress toward training, educational, and career goals.

Never   Infrequently   Sometimes   Frequently   Always

INSTRUCTIONS FOR SCORING AND
INTERPRETING: BUSINESS AND GOVERNMENT

1. The point value for each answer is listed below:

Never	1 point
Infrequently	2 points
Sometimes	3 points
Frequently	4 points
Always	5 points

2. Refer to the *Scoring Sheet: Business and Government* for the item statements of the scale (*Items* are identified with numbers) which are specifically listed under each of the six factors: Relationship Emphasis, Information Emphasis, Facilitative Focus, Confrontive Focus, Mentor Model, and Employee Vision.

3. Enter the point value (1 to 5 points) on the *Points* line which is below each of the numbered *Items*. For example, using "Factor 1: Relationship Emphasis," if you had circled as the answer to item statement "1" the word "Sometimes," then a "3" (points value) would be entered directly below the "1" on the *Scoring Sheet*. Then you would total all of the points recorded for "Factor 1" and enter the cumulative score on the (*total*) line.

4. After determining the total for each of the six separate factor item scores, then total *all* of the six separate factor scores and enter this overall score at the bottom of the sheet on the *Grand Total for Overall Score* line.

5. Refer to the *Mentor Role Competencies: Business and Government* chart. Enter the *Grand Total for Overall Score* in the appropriate block under *Overall Score*. Then enter the separate (*total*) score for each of the six factors in the appropriate block for the specific factor: Relationship Emphasis, Information Emphasis, Facilitative Focus, Confrontive Focus. Mentor Model, and Employee Vision.

6. Interpret scores in the ranges labeled *not effective* and *less effective* as indicating a need for professional improvement. A score

in the *effective* category indicates a general competency with opportunity for improvement. Interpret *very effective* and *highly effective* as indicating positive mentoring behavioral skills (which could still be fine tuned).

7. Refer to Appendix C: The Mentor Role: Six Behavioral Functions for the definition, purpose, and mentor behaviors associated with each of the six separate mentor functions. Consider all six of the mentor functions as a description of the complete (integrated) mentor role.

SCORING SHEET: BUSINESS AND GOVERNMENT

Factor 1: Relationship Emphasis

Items: 1, 5, 7, 12, 13, 23, 42, 44, 47, 53   *Relationship*

Points: __ __ __ __ __ __ __ __ __ __

                                                     (total)

Factor 2: Information Emphasis

Items: 3, 4, 6, 9, 10, 11, 19, 24, 40, 52   *Information*

Points: __ __ __ __ __ __ __ __ __ __

                                                     (total)

Factor 3: Facilitative Focus

Items: 15, 22, 25, 34, 39, 49   *Facilitative*

Points: __ __ __ __ __ __

                                                     (total)

Factor 4: Confrontive Focus

Items: 8, 16, 18, 21, 27, 31, 33, 37, 43, 46, 48, 51 *Confrontive*

Points: __ __ __ __ __ __ __ __ __ __ __ __

                                                     (total)

Factor 5: Mentor Model

Items: 2, 28, 29, 32, 36, 41   *Mentor*

Points: __ __ __ __ __ __

                                                     (total)

Factor 6: Employee Vision

Items: 14, 17, 20, 26, 30, 35, 38, 45, 50, 54, 55 *Employee*

Points: __ __ __ __ __ __ __ __ __ __ __

                                                     (total)

Grand Total for Overall Score: _____

MENTOR ROLE COMPETENCIES:
BUSINESS AND GOVERNMENT

Overall Score

55–176	177–192	193–206	207–222	223–275
not effective	less effective	effective	very effective	highly effective

Relationship Emphasis

10–34	35–37	38–40	41–43	44–50
not effective	less effective	effective	very effective	highly effective

Information Emphasis

10–31	32–35	36–37	38–41	42–50
not effective	less effective	effective	very effective	highly effective

Facilitative Focus

6–17	18–19	20–21	22–23	24–30
not effective	less effective	effective	very effective	highly effective

Confrontive Focus

12–33	34–37	38–41	42–46	47–60
not effective	less effective	effective	very effective	highly effective

Mentor Model

6–20	21	22–23	24–25	26–30
not effective	less effective	effective	very effective	highly effective

Employee Vision

11–33	34–36	37–39	40–43	44–55
not effective	less effective	effective	very effective	highly effective

APPENDIX C

The Mentor Role:
Six Behavioral Functions

The Mentor Role:
Six Behavioral Functions

1. *Relationship Emphasis*
Conveys through active, empathetic listening a genuine understanding and acceptance of the mentees' feelings

Purpose
To create a psychological climate of trust which allows mentees to honestly share and reflect upon their personal experiences (positive and negative) as adult learners

Mentor Behaviors
* Practice responsive listening (verbal and nonverbal reactions that signal sincere interest).
* Ask open-ended questions related to expressed immediate concerns about actual situations.
* Provide descriptive feedback based on observations rather than inferences of motives.
* Use perception checks to ensure comprehension of feelings.
* Offer nonjudgmental sensitive responses to assist in clarification of emotional states and reactions.

---

2. *Information Emphasis*
Directly requests detailed information from and offers specific suggestions to mentees about their current plans and progress in achieving personal, educational, and career goals

Purpose
To ensure that advice offered is based on accurate and sufficient knowledge of individual mentees

Mentor Behaviors

*Ask questions aimed at assuring factual understanding of present educational and career situation.

*Review relevant background to develop adequate personal profile.

*Ask probing questions which require concrete answers.

*Offer directive-type comments about present problems and solutions that should be considered.

*Make restatements to ensure factual accuracy and interpretive understanding.

*Rely on facts as an integral component of the decision-making process.

3. Facilitative Focus

Guides mentees through a reasonably in-depth review of and exploration of their interests, abilities, ideas, and beliefs

Purpose

To assist mentees in considering alternative views and options while reaching their own decisions about attainable personal, academic, and career objectives

Mentor Behaviors

*Pose hypothetical questions to expand individual views.

*Uncover the underlying experiential and information basis for assumptions.

*Present multiple viewpoints to generate a more in-depth analysis of decisions and options.

*Examine the seriousness of commitment to goals.

*Analyze reasons for current pursuits.

*Review recreational and vocational preferences.

4. Confrontive Focus

Respectfully challenges mentees' explanations for or avoidance of decisions and actions relevant to their development as adult learners

Purpose

To help mentees attain insight into unproductive strategies and behaviors and to evaluate their need and capacity to change

Mentor Behaviors

*Use careful probing to assess psychological readiness of the mentee to benefit from different points of views.

*Make an open acknowledgment of concerns about possible negative consequences of constructive ("critical") feedback on the relationship.

*Employ a confrontive verbal stance aimed at the primary goal of promoting self-assessment of apparent discrepancies.

*Focus on most likely strategies and behaviors for meaningful change.

*Use the least amount of carefully stated feedback necessary for impact.

*Offer comments (before and after confrontive remarks) to reinforce belief in positive potential for mentee growth beyond the current situation.

---

5. Mentor Model

Shares life experiences and feelings as a "role model" with mentees in order to personalize and enrich the relationship

Purpose

To motivate mentees to take necessary risks, to make decisions without certainty of successful results, and to overcome difficulties in the journey toward educational and career goals

Mentor Behaviors

*Offer personal thoughts and genuine feelings to emphasize the value of learning from unsuccessful or difficult experiences (as trial and error and self-correction, and not as growth-limiting "failures").

*Select related examples from own life (and experiences as mentor of other mentees) based on probable motivational value.

*Provide a direct, realistic assessment of positive belief in mentee's ability to pursue attainable goals.

*Express a confident view of appropriate risk taking as necessary for personal, educational, training, and career development.

*Make statements that clearly encourage personal mentee actions to attain stated objectives.

6. *Mentee Vision*
Stimulates mentees' critical thinking with regard to envisioning their own future and developing their personal and professional potential

Purpose
To encourage mentees as they manage personal changes and take initiatives in their transitions through life events as independent adult learners

Mentor Behaviors
*Make statements which require reflection on present and future educational, training, and career attainments.
*Ask questions aimed at clarifying perceptions (positive and negative) about personal ability to manage change.
*Review individual choices based on a reasonable assessment of options and resources.
*Make comments directed at analysis of problem-solving and decision-making strategies.
*Express confidence in carefully thought-out decisions.
*Offer remarks that show respect for mentees' capacity to determine their own future.
*Encourage mentees to develop talents and pursue dreams.

APPENDIX D

Information about the Principles
of Adult Mentoring Scale

Information about the Principles of Adult Mentoring Scale

ADJUSTMENT OF EACH VERSION FOR CONTEXT

The Principles of Adult Mentoring Scale has two versions: Postsecondary Education (PSE) and Business and Government (B&G). Each version has a separate set of scores for mentor role competencies, which are based on studies of the scales in the different worlds of education, and business and government. The degree to which the differences in the mentoring environment would probably influence the pursuit of such realistic concerns as personal, educational, training, and career development within the mentoring relationship are addressed within each version of the scale. However, the operational assumption is that the behavioral similarities of the effective mentor would be more important than the differences raised by the acknowledged challenges of context.

Version PSE includes more of a focus on the issues and resources expected in education, and version B&G includes more of an emphasis on the concerns associated with mentoring in business and government. Also, the scoring sheets for both factors and items and mentor role competencies contain either the descriptor "Student Vision" for PSE or "Employee Vision" for B&G.

MENTOR ROLE COMPETENCIES

The Mentor Role Competencies section for each version of the Principles of Adult Mentoring Scale provides an *Overall Score* for the complete mentor role based on an integrated composite of all six separate mentoring functions. Each of the six distinct behavioral functions—Relationship Emphasis, Information Emphasis,

Facilitative Focus, Confrontive Focus, Mentor Model, and Student or Employee Vision (depending on the version)—is also scored, but as a separate mentor competency.

A mentor may be proficient in some facets of mentoring and less effective in others, as indicated by the scoring continuum of *not effective, less effective, effective, very effective*, and *highly effective*. An implication of the scale is that *not effective* or *less effective* scores represent a potential negative impact on an adult learner as a consequence of experiencing the mentoring relationship. For example, a mentor who is actively confrontive but insufficiently attentive to relationship and informational concerns could detract rather than add to mentee development and learning.

The mentor effectiveness profile therefore reflects the degree of relative success as defined by the behavioral descriptions of mentor functions relevant to the overall mentor role and the six interdependent mentor functions. A summary explanation of the six behavioral functions of the mentor role is provided in Appendix C.

RELIABILITY

The reliability analysis provided coefficients for the Principles of Adult Mentoring Scale total scale score which showed an alpha of .9490 for the PSE version and an alpha of .9609 for the B&G version. The alpha score is computed on a scale between 0–1, and reveals the internal consistency of the item statements within a test. A total scale score approaching "1" would be viewed as indicating a high probability of reliability, which is demonstrated by the alpha scores for both versions of this scale.

Also, the Principles of Adult Mentoring Scale as a whole (all 55 item statements) was designed to measure the concept "mentoring," with each of the six scales measuring a distinct component of the mentoring relationship. For the scales to be considered as essentially related in that they all collectively measured *mentor behaviors*, each of the scales had to demonstrate positive correlation. The reliability analysis conducted of scale intercorrelations to determine if the six separate scales as a whole measured the construct "mentor behaviors" showed a high positive correlation for both versions of this scale, as indicated by the results of the Pearson Correlation Coefficient (r) data, which is the statistical procedure used to ascertain the extent of this relationship.

Additional information regarding the explanations offered above (Cohen, 1993), as well as other relevant statistics, including demographic profiles of the criterion group utilized to formulate scale normative scores for version B&G is available, and will be gladly furnished by the author. The Principles of Adult Mentoring Scale (both versions) is still being refined and studied to ensure that, as more relevant facts are accumulated regarding its application to mentoring, this updated data will be made available to the educational, business, and government community.

REFERENCES

Alleman, E. (1982). Mentoring relationships in organizations: Behaviors, personality characteristics, and interpersonal perceptions. *Dissertation Abstracts International.* (University Microfilms No. 86–05, 821)

Baskett, H. K., Marsick, V., & Cervero, R. (1992). Putting theory to practice and practice to theory. In H. K. Baskett & V. J. Marsick (Eds.), *Professionals' ways of knowing: New findings on how to improve professional education* (pp. 109–118). San Francisco: Jossey-Bass.

Beder, H. (1989). Purposes and philosophies of adult education. In S. B. Merriam & P. M. Cunningham (Eds.). *Handbook of adult and continuing education* (pp. 37–50). San Francisco: Jossey-Bass.

Belasco, J. (1991). *Teaching the elephant to dance: The manager's guide to empowering change.* New York: Penguin.

Bova, B. (1987). Mentoring as a learning experience. In V. J. Marsick (Ed.), *Learning in the workplace* (pp. 119–133). London: Croom Helm.

Brookfield, S. D. (1986). *Understanding and facilitating adult learning.* San Francisco: Jossey-Bass.

Brookfield, S. D. (1990). Discussion. In M. W. Galbraith (Ed.), *Adult learning methods* (pp. 187–204). Malabar, FL: Krieger.

Brookfield, S. D. (1991). Grounding teaching in learning. In M. W. Galbraith, (Ed.), *Facilitating adult learning: A transactional processes* (pp. 33–56). Malabar, FL: Krieger.

Charlesworth, E. A., & Nathan, R. G. (1982). *Stress management: A comprehensive guide to wellness.* New York: Ballantine.

Civikly, J. M. (1986). Meeting the challenge. In J. M. Civikly (Ed.), *Communicating in college classrooms* (pp. 93–98). New Directions for Teaching and Learning, no. 26. San Francisco: Jossey-Bass.

Cohen, N. H. (1993). The development and validation of the principles of adult mentoring scale for faculty mentors in higher education. *Dissertation Abstracts International.* (University Microfilms No. 9316468)

Covey, S. R. (1989). *The 7 habits of highly effective people.* New York: Simon & Schuster.

Daloz, L. A. (1986). *Effective teaching and mentoring: Realizing the transformational power of adult learning experiences.* San Francisco: Jossey-Bass.

Daloz, L. A. (1990). Mentorship. In M. W. Galbraith (Ed.), *Adult learning methods* (pp. 205–224). Malabar, FL: Krieger.

Devito, J. A. (1990). *Messages: Building interpersonal communication skills.* New York: Harper & Row.

Dewey, J. (1938). *Experience and education.* New York: MacMillan.

Fisher, R., & Ury, W. (1981). *Getting to yes: Negotiating agreement without giving in.* New York: Penguin.

Galbraith, M. W. (1990). Attributes and skills of an adult educator. In M. W. Galbraith (Ed.), *Adult learning methods* (pp. 3–22). Malabar, FL: Krieger.

Galbraith, M. W. (Ed.). (1991a). *Facilitating adult learning: A transactional process.* Malabar, Fl: Krieger.

Galbraith, M. W. (1991b). The adult learning transactional process. In M. W. Galbraith (Ed.), *Facilitating adult learning: A transactional process* (pp. 1–32). Malabar, FL: Krieger.

Galbraith, M. W. & Zelenak, B. S. (1991). Adult learning methods and techniques. In M. W. Galbraith (Ed.), *Facilitating adult learning: A transactional process* (pp. 103–133). Malabar, FL: Krieger.

Galbraith, M. W. & Zelenak, B. S. (1989). The education of adult and continuing education practitioners. In S. B. Merriam & P. Cunningham (Eds.), *Handbook of adult and continuing education* (pp. 124–133). San Francisco: Jossey-Bass.

Gaylin, W. (1992) *The male ego.* New York: Penguin.

Gilligan, C. (1982). *In a different voice: Psychological theory and women's development.* Cambridge: Harvard University Press.

Gray, W. A. (1991). *Mentoring products and services catalogue.* International Centre for Mentoring and the Mentoring Institute: West Vancouver, British Columbia, Canada, 6.

Hammond, D. C., Hepworth, D. H., & Smith, V. G. (1977). *Improving therapeutic communication.* San Francisco: Jossey-Bass.

Hanson, P. A. (1983). Protege perception of the mentor-protege relationships: Its complimentary nature and developmental tasks. *Dissertation Abstracts International.* (University Microfilms No. 83–23, 376)

Havighurst, R. J. (1972). *Developmental tasks and education.* New York: McKay.

Jacobi, M. (1991). Mentoring and undergraduate academic success: A literature review. *Review of Educational Research,* 61 (4), 505–532.

Jandt, F. E. (1985). *Win-win negotiating: Turning conflict into agreement.* New York: John Wiley & Sons.

Jeruchim, J., & Shapiro, P. (1992) *Women, mentors, and success*. New York: Fawcett Columbine.

Knowles, M. S. (1970). *The modern practice of adult education*. New York: Association Press.

Kram, K. (1985). *Mentoring at work*. Glenview, IL: Scott Foresman.

Levinson, D. J., Darrow, C. N., Klein, E., Levinson, M. H., & McKee, B. (1978). *The seasons of a man's life*. New York: Knopf.

Loughlin, K. A., & Mott, V. W. (1992). Models of women's learning: Implications for professional continuing education. In H. K. Morris & V. J. Marsick (Eds.), *Professionals' ways of knowing: New findings on how to improve professional education* (pp. 79–88). San Francisco: Jossey-Bass.

Marsick, V. J. (Ed.). (1987). *Learning in the workplace*. New York: Croom Helm.

Merriam, S. B. (1984). *Adult development: Implications for adult education*. Columbus, OH: ERIC Clearinghouse on Adult, Career, and Vocational Education.

Merriam, S. B. & Cunningham, P. M. (Eds.). (1989). *Handbook of adult and continuing education*. San Francisco: Jossey-Bass.

McGoldrick, M., Pearce, J. K., & Giordano, J. (1982). *Ethnicity & family therapy*. New York: The Guildford Press.

Miller, J. V., & Musgrove, M. J. (Eds.). (1986). *Issues in adult career counseling*. San Francisco: Jossey-Bass.

Murray, M. (1991). *Beyond the myths and magic of mentoring*. San Francisco: Jossey-Bass.

Naisbitt, J., & Aburdene, P. (1990). *Megatrends 2000*. New York: Avon.

Peters, T. (1987). *Thriving on chaos: Handbook for a management revolution*. New York: HarperCollins.

Rogers, C. A. (1961). *On becoming a person*. Boston: Houghton Mifflin.

Sayles. L. R. (1993). *The working leader*. New York: Macmillan.

Schlossberg, N. K. (1989) *Overwhelmed: Coping with life's ups and downs*. Lexington, MA: D. C. Heath & Co.

Schlossberg, N. K., Lynch, A. Q., & Chickering, A. W. (1989). *Improving higher education environments for adults*. San Francisco: Jossey-Bass.

Schon, D. B. (1987). *Educating the reflective practitioner*. San Francisco: Jossey-Bass.

Sheehy, G. (1981). *Pathfinders*. New York: Bantam.

Tannen, D. (1990). *You just don't understand: Women and men in conversation*. New York: Ballantine.

Theriot, R. (1986). Personality and behavioral characteristics of effective, average and ineffective mentor relationships. *Dissertations Abstracts International*. (University Microfilms No. 85–05, 821)

202 MENTORING ADULT LEARNERS

Thurston, A. S., & Robbins, W. A. (1983). (Eds.). *Counseling: A critical function for the 1980's*. San Francisco: Jossey-Bass.

Walter, J. L., & Peller, J. E. (1992). *Becoming solution-focused in brief therapy*. New York: Brunner/Mazel.

Weaver, R. L. (1993). *Understanding interpersonal communication*. New York: Harper Collins.

Williams, J. H. (1987). *Psychology of women*. New York: W. W. Norton & Co.

Witkin-Lanoil, G. (1984). *The female stress syndrome*. New York: Berkley

Witkin-Lanoil, G. (1986). *The male stress syndrome*. New York: Berkley.

Wlodkowski, R. J. (1990) Strategies to enhance adult motivation to learn. In M. W. Galbraith (Ed.), *Adult learning methods* (pp. 97–118). Malabar, FL: Krieger.

Zey, M. G. (1984). *The mentor connection*. Homewood, IL: Dow Jones-Irwin.

INDEX